ETRUSCAN
TOMB PAINTINGS

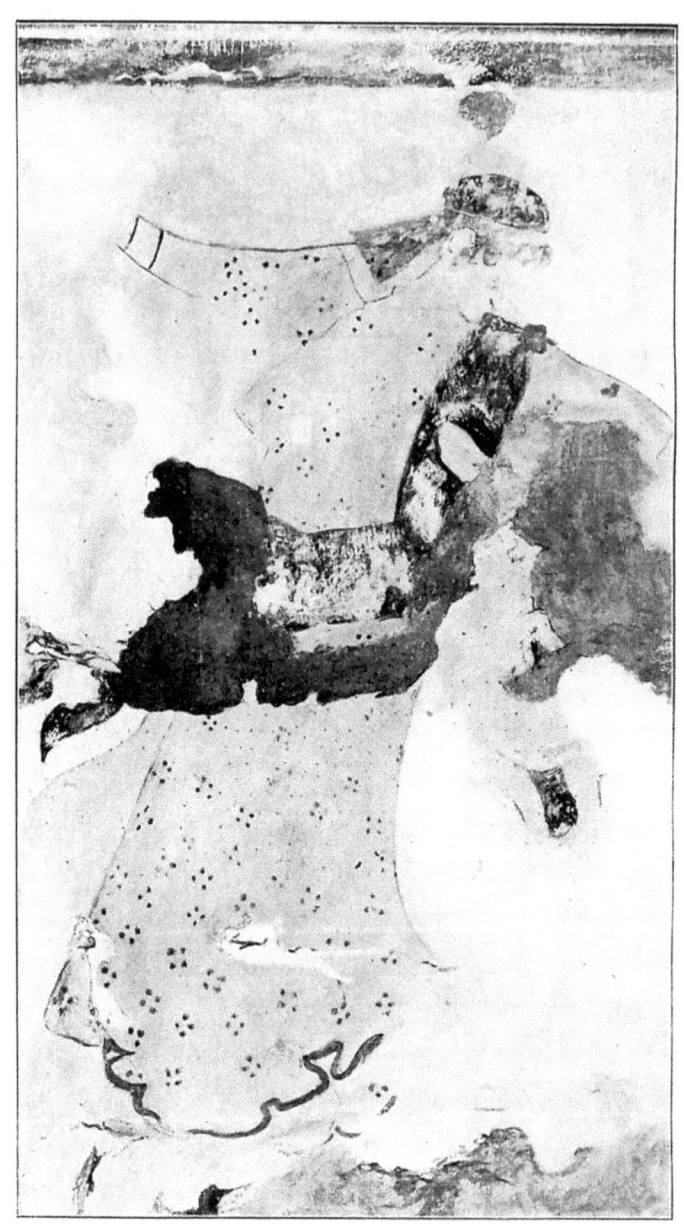

FIG. 11. 'LA BELLA BALLERINA' IN THE
TOMBA FRANCESCA GIUSTINIANI

After the facsimile of the Ny Carlsberg Glyptotek

ETRUSCAN TOMB PAINTINGS

THEIR SUBJECTS AND SIGNIFICANCE

BY

FREDERIK POULSEN

KEEPER OF THE CLASSICAL DEPARTMENT OF THE NY CARLSBERG GLYPTOTEK, COPENHAGEN
FELLOW OF THE DANISH ROYAL SOCIETY

TRANSLATED BY

INGEBORG ANDERSEN, M.A.

COACHWHIP PUBLICATIONS
CoachwhipBooks.com

Etruscan Tomb Paintings: Their Subjects and Significance, by Frederik Poulsen
First published 1922
© 2012 Coachwhip Publications

CoachwhipBooks.com

ISBN-13 978-1-61646-121-8

PREFACE

THE following sketch is based upon investigations made in the Etruscan Tombs at Corneto and Chiusi, and on comparison of the original wall-paintings with the facsimiles and drawings made from them and preserved in the Helbig Museum in the Ny Carlsberg Glyptotek. It was originally published in Danish, in 1919, as a guide to students in that Department.

I am greatly indebted to Mr. G. F. Hill, of the British Museum, for his revision of the translation.

Meanwhile the first volume of the promised work of Fritz Weege (*Etruskische Malerei*, Halle, 1921) has appeared, copiously and splendidly illustrated. The text contains general views concerning Etruscan religion and society rather than descriptions of the paintings themselves, and I cannot refrain from saying that I find Weege's statements and opinions, and the parallels which he adduces, too often more fanciful than convincing, in spite of the vast erudition displayed therein. I do not find anything in my own text which I feel inclined to alter after reading his book.

FREDERIK POULSEN.

COPENHAGEN,
January 1921.

LIST OF ILLUSTRATIONS

ETRUSCAN TOMB-PAINTINGS

I

THE tombs and tomb-paintings of Etruria constitute a field of archaeology in which the investigator is particularly apt to be reminded of numerous sins of omission and to be haunted by a painfully uneasy conscience. Indeed, the older archaeologists have less reason to plead guilty before the bar of science than those of more recent times. When the discovery and excavation of the Etruscan tombs began to make headway in the twenties of the nineteenth century, publications in text and illustrations followed comparatively close upon the discoveries. The first misfortune, however, took place when three of the most interesting tombs were published, the Tomba delle Bighe, the Tomba delle Iscrizioni, and the Tomba del Barone.

It was the major-domo of the Bishop of Corneto, Vittorio Masi, who first opened them together with other tombs in the vicinity of Corneto. In the spring of 1827 he invited two German barons, Stackelberg, an able archaeologist, and Kestner, the Hanoverian ambassador in Rome, to inspect them, and, if they so desired, to survey, draw, and publish the pictures in the tombs. The two men arrived, accompanied by Thürmer, a Bavarian architect, to find the tombs themselves despoiled of their accessories, but the walls covered with wonderful pictures dating from the sixth and fifth centuries B.C. They set to work immediately, studying and copying the pictures in the richest of the tombs, the Tomba delle Bighe. Stackelberg made five charming water-colours in order to save the colouring for posterity ; Thürmer executed eleven careful drawings. In all, the two men painted and drew two hundred and twenty-five figures, and the whole of the material is now preserved in the Archaeological

Seminar of the University of Strasburg. In his diary Stackelberg gives a vivid description of the discomfort which they experienced, drawing by torchlight in the cold, dank tomb-chamber, and only emerging now and then into the warm Italian spring sunlight in order to recuperate or to enjoy a light repast on the top of the tumulus, commanding a view of the sea. To this were added fatiguing social duties ; local patriotism was aroused in Corneto ; the noble families in the town vied in displaying hospitality to the Germans, and big banquets were held, at which sonnets were recited to the ' heroes ' who once slept in the tombs. The drawing and copying of the colours on the walls in the Tomb of the Chariots, as well as in the Tomb of the Inscriptions and in the Tomb of the Baron—so called after Baron Kestner— were rightly considered the chief matter, because in the very first summer after they were opened, the dampness of the tombs in a few weeks ruined large portions of them, especially in the Tomba delle Bighe. After his return to Rome, Baron Stackelberg caught typhoid fever and did not recover till late in the winter. In the next spring he went to Germany, where his excavations had created such an immense sensation that even the aged Goethe asked Stackelberg to dine with him in Weimar and studied the drawings with the greatest interest. But, in spite of the national enthusiasm called forth by the excavations, the projected great work came to nothing ; the coloured plates of the paintings, with the then existing means of reproduction, promised to be so expensive that the publishers took alarm. Pending these negotiations, the paintings from the three tombs were published in French and Italian works in very poor and incorrect reproductions, and no other reproductions were available till 1916, when the German archaeologist, Weege, at last managed to bring out an admirable publication of the Tomba delle Bighe, the most important of the three tombs.[1]

Similar uncoloured, not very reliable drawings continued to be the method of reproducing the Etruscan tomb-paintings

[1] *Jahrbuch des deutschen archäologischen Instituts*, xxxi. 1916, p. 106 ff.

in the following decades ; after these drawings were made the reproductions in handbooks like Jules Martha's *L'Art étrusque* (Paris, 1889). An Englishman, George Dennis, in his *Cities and Cemeteries of Etruria* (London, 1878), gives a vivid description of Tuscan scenery and of the ancient tombs. At times he rises to a lyrical enthusiasm ; for instance, in his description of a dancing figure, ' la bella ballerina di Corneto ', in the Tomba Francesca Giustiniani. But neither Dennis nor any later visitor procured copies which come up to their enthusiasm ; in fact, the beautiful ballerina has never even been drawn or photographed, and is not to be found in any work on archaeology or art. Dennis's book throws a dreadful light upon contemporary excavation. About Veii, he writes that the greater part of the district belongs to the Queen of Sardinia, who in the excavating season positively lets out tracts of land to Roman dealers, who rifle the tombs of everything convertible into cash and then cover them in with earth. He describes such an excavation at Vulci : a tomb being opened, nothing but pottery was found ; the excavators, in their disgust, smashed and destroyed everything, in spite of the English traveller's protests and entreaties. This took place on the estate of the Princess of Canino.[1]

This happened in the sixties. In the seventies such vandalism comes to an end ; but the publications do not improve. For example, in the excellent article on the Tomba François at Vulci which Körte published in the *Archäologisches Jahrbuch* for 1897, the illustrations are poor : and it was not until 1907 that Körte published, in the second volume of the *Antike Denkmäler*, beautiful coloured reproductions of the paintings in three tombs at Corneto, the Tomba dei Tori, the Tomba delle Leonesse, and the Tomba della Pulcella. A popular description by Mary Lovett Cameron, *Old Etruria and Modern Tuscany* (London, 1909), marks no progress as far as the illustrations are concerned, and the text is amateurish and superficial.[2] Von Stryk's

[1] *Cities and Cemeteries*, p. 119.
[2] The same is true of the second edition of Luigi Dasti's *Notizie di Tarquinia-Corneto*, 1910.

dissertation, *Die etruskischen Kammergräber*, published at Dorpat in 1910, is unillustrated : the text is full of errors, and in the discursive descriptions no account is taken of the difference between the present state of the tomb-paintings and that revealed by the earlier publications. Weege's above-mentioned article on the Tomba delle Bighe and the Tomba dei Leopardi only appeared in 1916 : here at last the entire material is utilized—the old drawings and descriptions, modern photographs, and the author's own careful notes. According to a prospectus recently issued, a larger work on Etruscan tomb-paintings, by the same author, is shortly to appear ; it will be awaited with interest.

It is to be hoped that Mr. Weege's book will supply a want which is felt the more acutely when we consider the growing interest in antique painting displayed in the last decades. In 1904 Furtwängler, with the assistance of the painter Reichhold, began the publication of the great work on the masterpieces of Greek vase-painting (*Griechische Vasen-malerei*), which was continued by Hauser : part of the third volume is now published. In 1906 appeared the first instal-ment of Paul Hermann's great collection of plates after antique, especially Pompeian, wall-painting ; this work, which is still in progress, contains beautiful reproductions with and without colours (*Denkmäler der Malerei des Alter-tums*). Finally, in 1914, Walther Riezler published a splendid work on the white Attic lekythoi (*Weissgründige attische Lekythen*). But during these years nobody thought of bringing to light the treasures hidden away in the sepulchral chambers of Corneto, Chiusi, and Orvieto, although these pictures were much more exposed to destruction than either the vases in the well-guarded rooms of the Museums or the Pompeian wall-paintings. For after heavy showers the floors of the deeply sunk tombs of Corneto are under water, and the damp then loosens the tufa of the walls so that the layer of stucco, on which the colours are laid *al fresco*, peels off. The heavy iron doors which the Italian Government has placed before the entrances are worse than useless, because they shut the moisture in and prevent the tombs from getting dry. If these doors had been placed at the top of the stairs leading to the tombs, thus changing place with the lattice doors which are now there, all would have been well. At Corneto, it is moisture which demolishes the stucco layer, varying from $\frac{1}{4}$ to 1 cm. in thickness, and bleaches the colours—red chalk, vermilion, lime-colour, ochre, cobalt, and copper colours, at Chiusi it is the drought which most frequently destroys the paintings, the colours here being laid directly on the stone walls.

We have, therefore, every reason to be deeply grateful to the late Carl Jacobsen who, at the beginning of the nineties, had the Etruscan tomb-paintings facsimiled on their actual scale. A somewhat similar experiment had already been tried, and the result is a number of facsimiles preserved in the Museo Gregoriano of the Vatican, but these are more decorative than exact. At first, the Italian painters, to whom Helbig, at the request of Carl Jacobsen, entrusted the task—the first was Marozzi—evidently imagined that Carl Jacobsen wanted these paintings as mural decorations for his museum and had no artistic or scientific aim in view, and letters from Helbig show that, as late as 1895, he did not scruple to let Becchi, the painter, fill in a damaged head from a picture in the Tomba dei Vasi Dipinti after the reproduction in *Monumenti*, vol. ix (1870). The first copies sent to the Ny Carlsberg Glyptotek were therefore of the same ' picture-postcard ' colouring as the earlier ones in the Museo Gregoriano, but gradually Carl Jacobsen increased the rigour of his demands for conscientious exactitude, and the facsimiles now on exhibition in the Helbig Museum of the Ny Carlsberg Glyptotek are almost all executed according to the more modern and better principles of copying. To be sure, these copies still leave a great deal to be desired in the way of scientific exactitude ; I have been able myself to ascertain this by a careful comparison with notes taken from the originals in the tombs of Corneto, and Weege more especially has pointed out rather grave mistakes in the copies of the paintings from the Tomba delle Bighe. But these may be supplemented by a series of beautiful coloured drawings dating from the last years of Jacobsen's life : they are framed and constitute a whole picture-book open to the public in the Helbig Collection. A large number of ground plans and decorative details are included in these drawings, in addition to the most important of the paintings, and here the copying has been executed with great accuracy. The Ny Carlsberg Glyptotek, then, thanks to Carl Jacobsen, is the place where investigators can most easily form an idea of the development of Etruscan wall-painting, far more easily than in Florence where the late Director, Milani, ordered new copies which, in my opinion, are considerably inferior to those of Carl Jacobsen. But for all that, the facsimiles of the Ny Carlsberg Glyptotek ought not to be the last word of science on the subject. Mr. Weege proposes, as the method of the future, the taking in the tombs themselves of gigantic photographs on which careful painters might add the colouring; instead of two there will thus only be one possibility of distortion, namely, in the colours themselves. But one might perhaps go still further and take large chromatic photographs which would fix both forms and colours for all time, so that we might view the gradual destruction of the originals with less dismay than at present.

A detailed estimate of the *artistic* significance and properties of the Etruscan wall-paintings is not yet possible, if only because no adequate pictures for reproduction exist. What can be done—and what will be attempted in the following pages—is to give an account of the content of the pictures and of the main lines of their development. Even that is not superfluous. Investigators have never really given themselves time to enter deeply into the spirit and content of these pictures, or to ask themselves the question which arises, one may say, with every picture, namely, how far the representation is a loan from Greek art and civilization, and how far it bears the local Etruscan stamp.

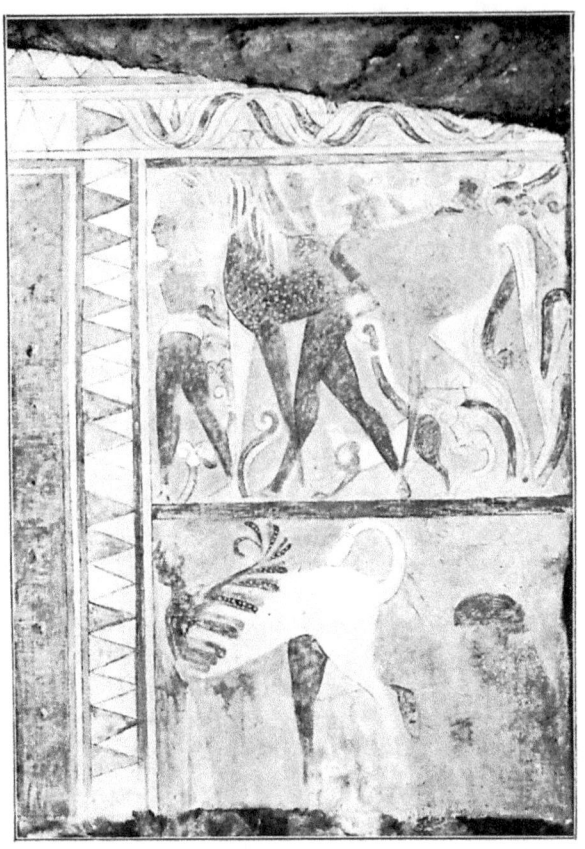

Fig. 1

WALL-PAINTING FROM THE TOMBA CAMPANA

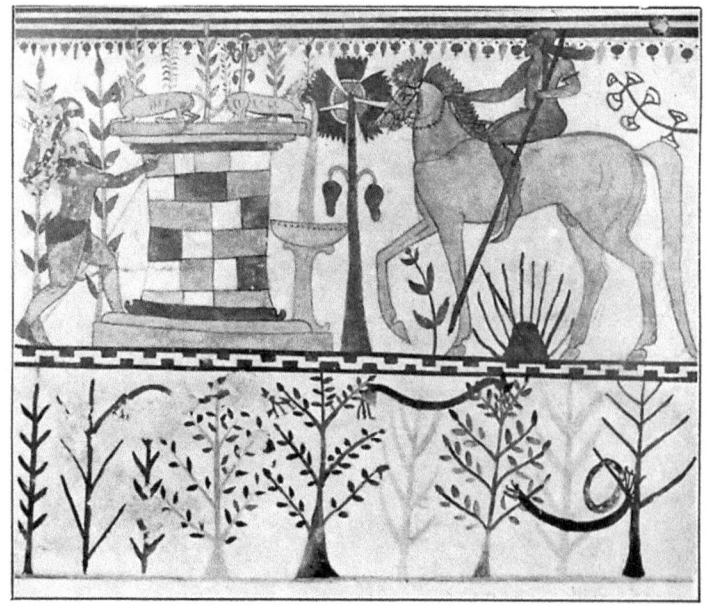

Fig. 2

MAIN PICTURE IN THE TOMBA DEI TORI AT CORNETO

II

THE first stage of development is represented by the Tomba Campana at Veii. This tomb was discovered in 1843, and a good description of it is given by Canina in *Antica Città di Veii* (1847), but it has never been published with adequate illustrations. A new and thorough treatment of the ornamentation and motives of its pictures is given in a Leipzig dissertation by Andreas Rumpf (*Die Wandmalereien in Veii*, 1915). But this, too, is without illustrations. The central doorway of the back wall is provided with an ornamental painted border and flanked by paintings in yellow, grey, and red on a blue ground. The work is primitive. The ornamentation is akin to that of Greek vase-painting of the seventh century B.C. The pictures are purely decorative : animals and fabulous animals such as lion, sphinx, deer, and panther fill the surface side by side with lotus-flowers and palmettes. There is no narrative element. To be sure, Weege, like others before him, has tried to construe one of the pictures (fig. 1) into a mythological scene : the boy on the horse, which is led by the bridle by a man walking behind, is thought to be a dead man on his way to Hades, and the man with the loin-cloth, carrying an axe over his shoulder, to the left in front of the horse, to be the Etruscan death-god and conductor of souls, Charun, to whom we shall return later. Weege also thinks that the animal crouching on the back of the horse is a hunting leopard. But, apart from the rather puzzling question, what the hunting leopard has to do with the ride to Hades, the animal is not a hunting leopard at all : it is a feline animal with a short tail, while the hunting leopard has a long tail. The animal was only placed there to fill up the space, thus illustrating the poverty of ideas in these pictures. Moreover, as the man with the axe is not characterized as Charun, either by colour or by dress, it seems unnecessary to force a mythological explanation. The human figures in this picture, as in the Melian vases of the seventh century B.C., are purely decorative : they ride when the space above the back of the horse has to be filled in, and they walk when a long, narrow field makes the human figure more appropriate than a seated or walking animal as a means of filling the space. The absurd alternation of colours within the same figure, every single animal being coloured in compartments of yellow and red and having alternately red and yellow legs, affords a good instance of purely decorative conception and suggests the idea of woven tapestry. Hence it is an all but obvious conclusion to imagine, as prototype of this painting, some magnificently coloured wall-tapestry imported into Etruria in the seventh century B.C. from Crete or one of the islands in the Aegean Sea, to the vase-paintings of which the ornamentation of the tomb shows close affinity.[1] Thus there is in these pictures neither any action nor any reference to death or the tomb. They serve as a decorative ornamentation of the tomb-chamber, like the six painted shields in the inner chamber of the tomb, which suggest those ' brass circles ' mentioned by Livy (VIII, 20, 8) as common votive offerings in early Rome. We can imagine the home of a rich Etruscan in the seventh century decorated with similar frescoes : painted tapestries and painted shields as substitutes for real wall-tapestries and metal shields.[2] The Tomba Campana is the most impressive but not the only representative of this earliest class of tombs, in the ornamentation of which only decorative considerations have been kept in view. Tombs at Cosa, Chiusi, Magliano, and Caere contain still more primitive paintings of the same sort, but they are badly preserved and still more imperfectly described.[3]

[1] Cp. Fr. Poulsen, *Der Orient und die frühgriechische Kunst*, p. 128, where I tried to prove that the pictures of the tomb are influenced by the art and style of decoration of the island of Cyprus. Rumpf (*op. cit.* 50) was nearer the mark in perceiving the connexion with the decorative art of Crete and the Cyclades in the seventh century B.C. The horsemen, in particular, recall the frieze from Prinia in Crete, *Bollettino d'Arte*, 1908, p. 457 ff.

[2] Shields were also common mural decorations with the early Greeks, cp. Poulsen, *Orient*, p. 77, and Alcaeus, *fragm* 15 (Bergk).

[3] See the summary account in Rumpf, *op. cit.* 61 ff.

III

THE next stage in the development is represented by the Tomba dei Tori at Corneto, discovered in 1892 and admirably published by G. Körte in *Antike Denkmäler*.[1] The back wall of the main chamber in this tomb has two doors, and it is between these that the one large figure painting is placed, again in such a way as to suggest a tapestry stretched on the wall (fig. 2). But now the picture has a narrative content, inasmuch as a scene from the Greek cycle of myths is depicted: Achilles watches for the Trojan prince Troilus at a well. Achilles, to the left, wears a crested Corinthian helmet, sword, greaves, and red loin-cloth. Troilus is naked and only decorated with armlets and elegant shoes. He wears his hair long, according to Ionic fashion, and in his hand he carries a goad (kentron). This is, as a rule, only used when two horses are ridden, and the drawing shows traces of double contours near the head and the right leg of the horse ; it is probable, therefore, that two horses were originally planned. In this picture also, the proportions of man and horse are impossible, but progress is perceptible in the monochromatic treatment of the body and legs of the horse. On the other hand, the old manner of painting in stripes or compartments is still retained in the running chimera in the pediment above ; it also lingers for a very long time in the pedimental figures of the following period. The style is Ionic of the first half of the sixth century B.C. A truly Ionian monster, created under Oriental influence, is the human-faced bull in the pediment above the door, one of the two bulls from which the tomb derives its name, and which are omitted here because of the obscene groups on either side of them. Other decorative details point to Cyrene and Egypt, especially the characteristic frieze of lotuses and pomegranates, which corresponds with the Cyrenaic vases of the sixth century B.C., and the stylized flower-bed under the

[1] II, Tafel 41, and Hilfstafel 1–8.

belly of the horse, which has its origin in Egyptian and its parallels in Phoenician and in orientalizing Greek art.[1] In this tomb the painting is not executed *al fresco* but in a yellowish-white pigment which unfortunately scales off in large flakes.

Thus in the Tomba dei Tori, besides a decorative treatment of the wall surface with friezes, we have a main picture with a mythological subject, painted in the Greek spirit and perhaps actually executed by a Greek mural painter. We do not find even the slightest allusion to death or entombment, or the least trace of any Etruscan characteristics. The inscription in the large frieze is of interest because it shows the Etruscan language in its archaic form, with a rich vocalization which must have made it much more euphonious than the language spoken later, in the fourth or following centuries. The inscription runs : ' arnth spuriana s[uth]il hece ce fariceka,' and means, ' Aruns Spurinna monumentum sepulcrale . . . condidit, adornavit,' or the like.[2]

IV

A CONSIDERABLE group of Etruscan tomb-paintings, dating from the middle of the sixth century, show in their composition close connexion with Ionic vase-painting, especially with the so-called Caeretan hydriae, while their main pictures tell us something about the Etruscans themselves and their conceptions of Life and Death and Eternity. Only in the animal friezes beneath the painted roof-supports does the old decorative conception of the human and animal figure still linger ; elsewhere the pictures now have content and meaning.

We may take the Tomba degli Auguri in Corneto,

[1] Poulsen, *Orient*, p. 67.
[2] I am greatly indebted to Professor O. A. Danielsson of Upsala for information about this as well as about other inscriptions, and for numerous linguistic suggestions on the general subject of my treatise.

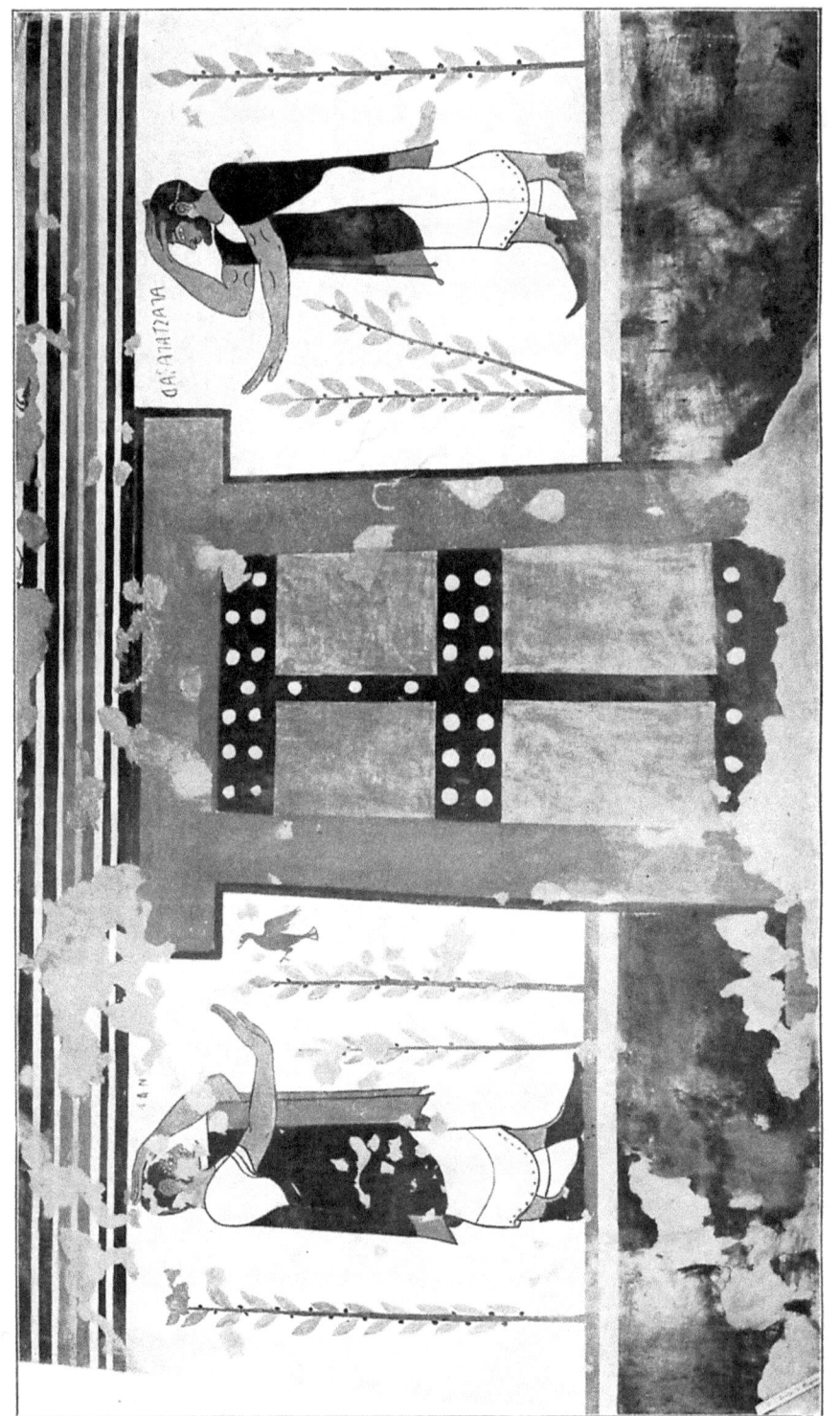

Fig. 3. BACK WALL IN THE TOMBA DEGLI AUGURI

discovered in 1878, as our starting-point. There are coloured
drawings as well as full-sized facsimiles of its pictures in the
Helbig Museum.

The middle of the back wall of this tomb is occupied by
a painted door flanked by two men in white chitons and
short black cloaks lined with red ; on their feet are peaked
shoes. They raise both arms in a gesture of lament, ' beating
their foreheads ' as the ancient texts have it.[1] With this
scene (fig. 3) the key-note is struck : the living stand at the
door of the tomb and moan for the dead, a subject specially
appropriate to the decoration of the walls of a tomb.

The scenes on the main walls are also associated with the
funeral ceremonies. On the right-hand main wall (fig. 4) a
boy is seen to the left in a white tunic with black dots, carrying
a stool and raising one arm and his face to a man who, dressed
in a red and brown cloak and brown shoes, seems to beckon
to the boy with his right hand, gesticulating at the same time
with his left. Between them a small figure is seated who
reminds one of the small boys in the Greek tomb reliefs
' weeping on their cold knees '. To the right is another man
clad in chiton and mantle, gesticulating violently with his
left hand, and carrying a crook in his right. Above him, and
above the excited man to the right, runs the inscription :
' Tevarath ', probably meaning umpire ($\beta\rho\alpha\beta\epsilon\upsilon\tau\acute{\eta}s$, $\acute{\alpha}\gamma\omega\nu o$-
$\theta\acute{\epsilon}\tau\eta s$). For now follow representations of athletic contests :
two wrestlers engaging in the initial grips, the elder bearded,
the younger beardless : between them are seen the prizes—
metal bowls ; these are supposed to be arranged in the
background, but owing to the lack of perspective they seem
to be in the way of the combatants. This scene throws light
on the preceding one : the man with the crook is evidently
not an augur, as originally conjectured because of the staff
and the flying birds, but the umpire who has to see that no
unfair tricks are used ; the other man is the spectator who

[1] $\Pi\alpha\acute{\iota}\epsilon\iota\nu$ $\tau\grave{\alpha}$ $\mu\acute{\epsilon}\tau\omega\pi\alpha$, Dionys. Hali-   see Sittl, *Gebärden der Griechen und*
carn. x. 9 ; ' frontem ferire ', Cicero,   *Römer*, p. 21.
Epist. ad Attic. i. 1 ; for other instances

has not yet seated himself, but beckons to the slave-boy to bring him the stool on which he will sit down like the Roman knights of later times who brought their own stools into the orchestra of the theatre. On the other hand, the mourning, crouching slave-boy seems to repeat the death lament of the back wall. Here already, then, we can observe the curious fragmentariness of the scenes in Etruscan art : they look as if they had been cut out of more comprehensive wholes, and put together without logical sequence. Clarity and unity are wanting. There is not the sustained composition or the pleasure in detailed narrative which are regular in Greek and Egyptian art. The Etruscan artist is content with hints and fragments.

To the right of the wrestlers, on the same main wall, is a particularly interesting representation : beneath the inscription Phersu, a man, dressed and masked like a punchinello, is leading a dog in a long leash which is wound round his antagonist and ends in a wooden collar round the neck of the dog. The ferocious blood-hound has inflicted bleeding wounds on the legs and thighs of the antagonist, and the antagonist, whose head is muffled in a sack, is vainly trying to disentangle himself from the leash and to hit the dog with a club. The explanation of this exciting and brutal contest, to which no parallel can be found in Greek art, is evidently that Phersu tries to make his dog bite his antagonist to death before the latter can get his head out of the sack and hit man and dog with his club. If the club-bearer succeeds in freeing himself from the sack and the dog, Phersu has only one chance : to run away. As runner, he has his legs stiffened with thongs, and in the much damaged fresco on the left main wall of the tomb we see the flight of Phersu (fig. 5) and (not reproduced) the club-bearer pursuing him. They are separated by a pair of pugilists who are boxing to the accompaniment of flutes, again an evidence of Etruscan indifference to incongruities in the composition. The escaping Phersu is painted alone in another tomb at Corneto, the Tomba del Pulcinella, the name of which is derived from this figure, but

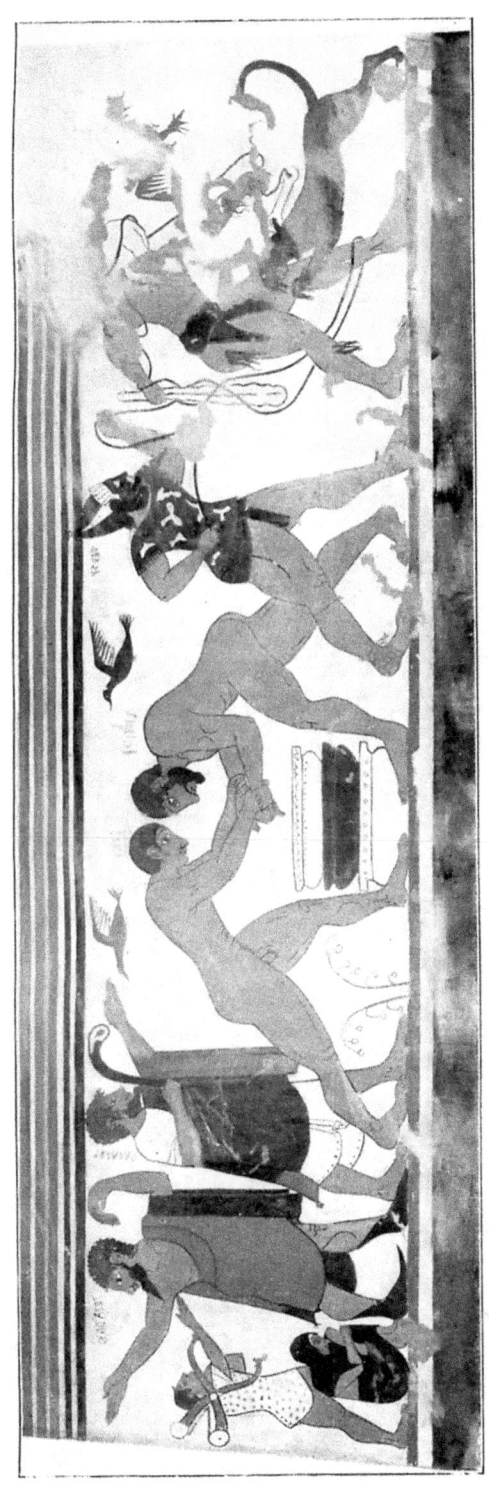

FIG. 4. RIGHT MAIN WALL IN THE TOMBA DEGLI AUGURI

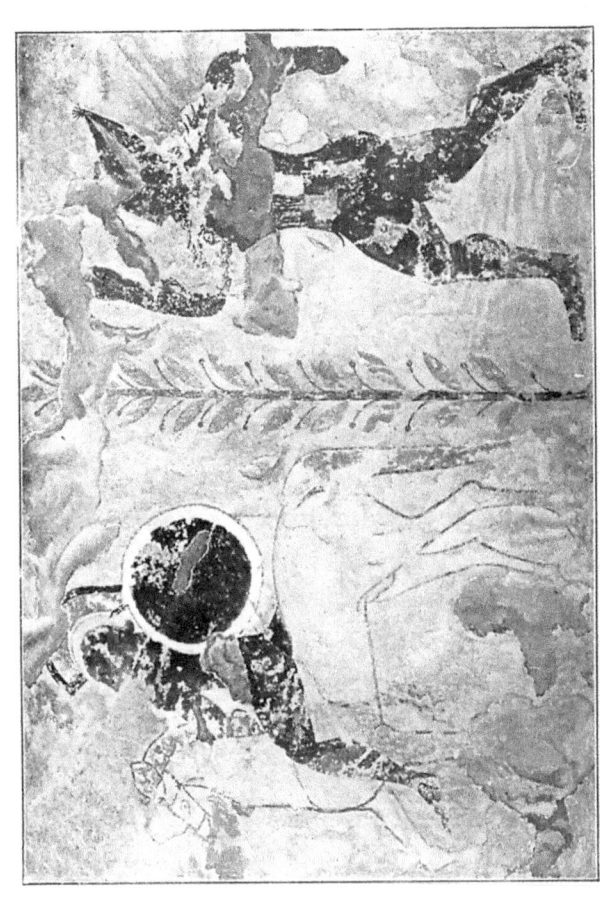

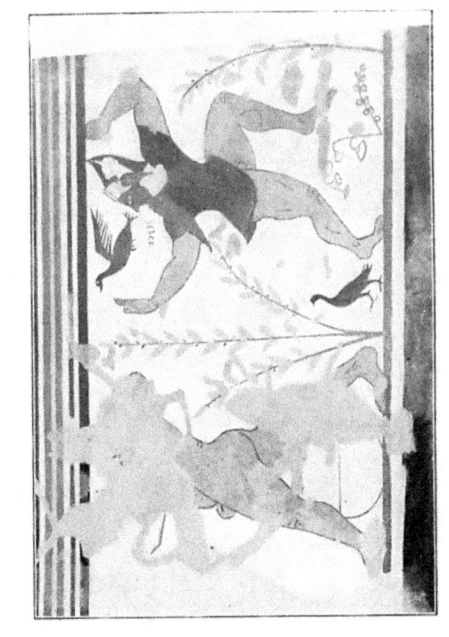

FIG. 6. PAINTING FROM THE TOMBA DEL PULCINELLA

FIG. 5. PART OF THE LEFT MAIN WALL
IN THE TOMBA DEGLI AUGURI
After a coloured drawing in the Helbig Museum

here he is placed beside a horseman (fig. 6), who represents the equestrian processions at funerals, to which we shall turn our attention later. The Tomba del Pulcinella, which was discovered in 1872, also dates from the sixth century B.C., and like the Tomb of the Augur it bears the stamp of Ionic art, especially in the receding contours of the crown of the head and in the plump forms of the body.

In these two sepulchres, then, we are confronted with representations which are associated not only with death and the tomb, but also with Etruscan local customs and national character. It is true that prize-fights and wrestling contests in connexion with obsequies are known in the Greek civilized world as well, for instance from the description in the *Iliad* of the funeral of Patroclus, and lingered for a long time especially in the outskirts of the Greek world—thus King Nicocles of Cyprus, in the beginning of the fourth century B.C., honoured his deceased father with choral dancing, athletic games, horse-races, trireme races.[1] But we know of no example from Hellas of a fight like that between Phersu, accompanied by his blood-hound, and the muffled club-bearer: a fight the attraction of which, apart from its sanguinary character, evidently depended on the disparity of the weapons, as it did in the combat between gladiator and retiarius, the man armed with net and trident, in the Roman arenas of a later day.[2]

From the Greek author Athenaeus,[3] we learn that the gladiatorial games originated in Campania, where they were introduced as entertainments at banquets, but that the Romans adopted them from the Etruscans. This tradition is confirmed by the facts that the name applied to the leader and trainer of the Roman gladiatorial school, *lanista*, is of Etruscan origin, and that the person, who even in late Rome [4] dragged the corpses from the arena, the so-called *Dispater*,

[1] Isocrates ix. 1.

[2] With reference to *phersu*, which is supposed to be synonymous with and the origin of the Latin *persona*, see Pauly-Wissowa, vi. 775, and S. P. Cortsen, *Vocabulorum Etruscorum interpretatio* in *Nord. Tidsskr. for Filologi*, 1917, p. 174.

[3] iv. 153 f.

[4] Tertullian, *Ad nation.* i. 10.

was furnished with satyr-ears and a mask with savage features, and carried a hammer, thus being a faithful copy of the Etruscan death-god, Charun.[1] Moreover, as the Etruscans in the heyday of their glory, in the sixth and fifth centuries B.C., also ruled over Campania, it is most natural to attribute to them, and not to the Campanian Graeculi, the doubtful honour of being the actual ' inventors ' of gladiatorial combats. These combats were a piquant and exciting substitute for actual human sacrifices in honour of the deceased noble or the gods, and as one of the parties was given a chance to save his life the practice may even be considered an advance in humanity.

Etruscan obscurity and inconsistency lead to curious confusion in the transition from mythological pictures to funereal scenes. Thus we find on the front of an early archaic Etruscan terra-cotta sarcophagus, now in the British Museum,[2] a representation in relief, manifestly inspired by Greek mythology, of a battle scene with men and women as spectators ; at one end of the sarcophagus, the left, leave-taking before marching out to battle ; on the back, a banqueting-scene, evidently representing the funeral feast, since the relief on the other end of the sarcophagus shows four mourning women, two of them holding drinking-bowls in their hands.

V

A GOOD idea of the different sort of athletic contests at the great Etruscan funerals is given by the wall-paintings in the Tomba delle Iscrizioni at Corneto, described and copied by Stackelberg and Kestner in 1827,[3] and represented in the Ny Carlsberg Glyptotek by facsimiles and coloured drawings executed in 1907, after a chemical treatment of the plaster stucco, which brought out a number of details more plainly.

[1] Pauly-Wissowa, iii. 2178.   *Sarcophagi in British Museum*, pl. ix–xi.
[2] B 630. Figured in *Terra-cotta*   [3] Kestner, *Annali* i (1829), p. 101 ff.

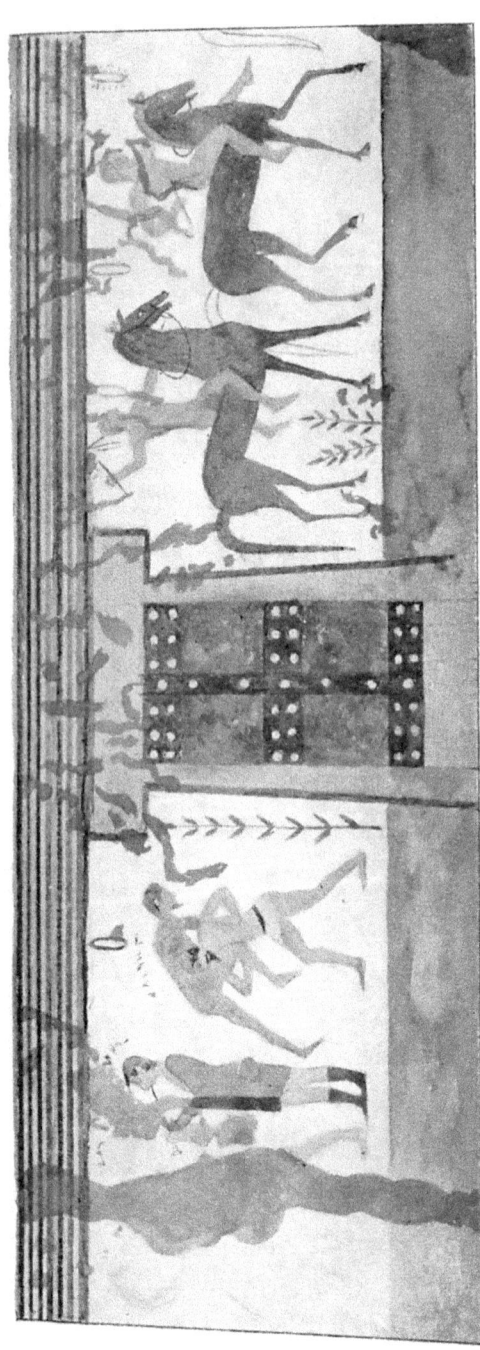

FIG. 7. LEFT MAIN WALL OF THE TOMBA DELLE ISCRIZIONI. After a coloured drawing in the Helbig Museum

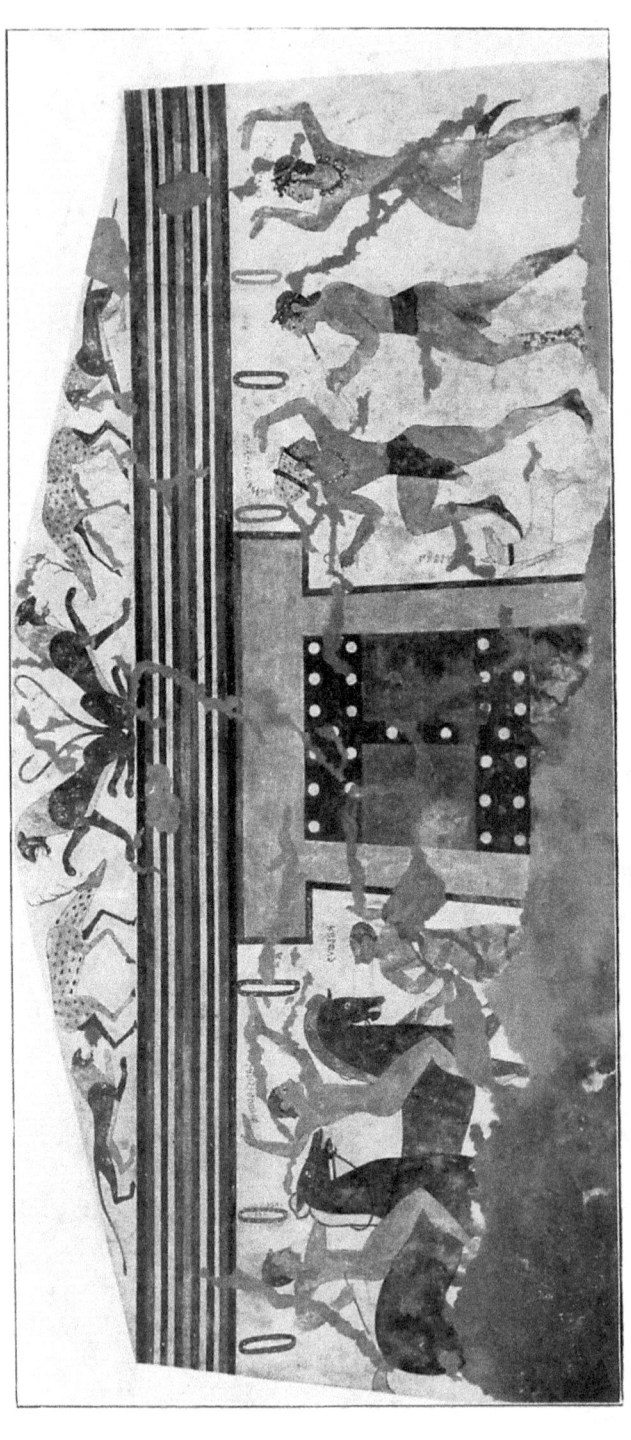

FIG. 8. BACK WALL OF THE TOMBA DELLE ISCRIZIONI

The pictures are of the same period as those of the Augur tomb, and of similar style. The numerous inscriptions from which the tomb has derived its title seem to be mostly proper names. Each of the three wall-surfaces of this tomb, which contains only one chamber, has a false painted door in the middle. Of the first figures on the left main wall, two pugilists, only very little is preserved (fig. 7). They are contending, like the two wrestlers to the right of them, one of whom has lifted the other from the ground, to the accompaniment of the flute-player who is standing between the two groups. This and many other Etruscan paintings confirm the statement of Aristotle[1] that the Etruscans made their boxers perform to the sound of the flute. Flute-playing was so popular that masters scourged their slaves and caused their cooks to work in the kitchen to the sound of the flute ; and here again the Romans adopted the Etruscan tradition and gave their flute-players a recognized position in the community, as is shown by the amusing story about the strike of the Roman flute-players[2] : the flute-players left Rome in disgust and went in a body to Tibur, and the only device the Romans could think of was to make the excellent fellows drunk and cart them back to Rome, where the citizens made haste to confirm the ancient privileges of the flute-players and to add several new ones in order to make the awakening more pleasant.

On the other side of the false door the equestrian procession begins and is continued on the back wall to the central false door (fig. 8). Four young naked horsemen, some of them with staves in their hands, are received by a naked youth who carries a palm-branch over his shoulder. Apart from the nakedness, which must be attributed to the influence of Greek art, this equestrian procession is genuinely Etruscan. Appian derives the festive processions at triumphs and funerals from Etruscan prototypes, while Dionysius of Halicarnassus finds their prototypes in Hellas. But it cannot be denied that Dionysius's description of these *pompae* in early

[1] Athenaeus iv. 154a.   [2] Livy ix. 30. 5–10. Plutarch, *Aetia Romana*, 55.

Rome [1] suggests Etruria : first came young horsemen, then foot-soldiers ; after these, athletes with their sexual organs covered (in contrast to Greek custom), then the tripartite chorus of dancers in purple cloaks and bronze belts, then the grotesque dancers, flute-players, lyre-players, and thurifers, and finally the procession of chariots with the images of the gods. In the following pages we shall make acquaintance with all these groups in the Etruscan world of art.

The equestrian procession is presumably the preliminary to a horse-race. The nobles of Etruria were celebrated for their race-horses and often sent their chariot-teams to the games in early Rome.[2] It is a characteristic fact that one of the few Etruscan words given by the Greek lexicographer Hesychius is no other than the word for horse, δάμνος according to the Greek version.[3]

To the right of the false door in the back wall three jolly dancers are seen : the first has his brow wreathed, carries a drinking-bowl in hand, and wears boots, red skirt, and blue neckerchief. The figure is shown by the flesh tint to be male, not female as stated in Carl Jacobsen's catalogue. After him dances the flute-player, with red boots, blue loin-cloth, and red chaplet, and last comes a naked dancing youth with boots, necklace, and chaplet.

Dancers appear in a number of Etruscan tomb-paintings, and abandon themselves to their gambols with a frenzy which might seem incompatible with death and entombment. In the Tomba del Morto at Corneto, dating from the same period, we find traces of a pirouetting dancer close to the couch of the dead and the lamenting mourners ; the dance was thus as important as the funeral lament (fig. 9). The finest representations of Etruscan mourning dancers are found in the Tomba del Triclinio, which dates from the beginning of the fifth century B.C. : the Ny Carlsberg Glyp-

[1] Dionys. Halicarn. vii. 72–3.
[2] Livy i. 35. 9.
[3] Hesych. s. v. The word is not mentioned in S. P. Cortsen's *Voca-bulorum Etruscorum interpretatio* in *Nordisk Tidsskr. for Filologi*, 1917 ; no doubt because he considers Hesychius's statement insufficiently authoritative. Cp. Skutsch, Pauly-Wissowa, vi. 775.

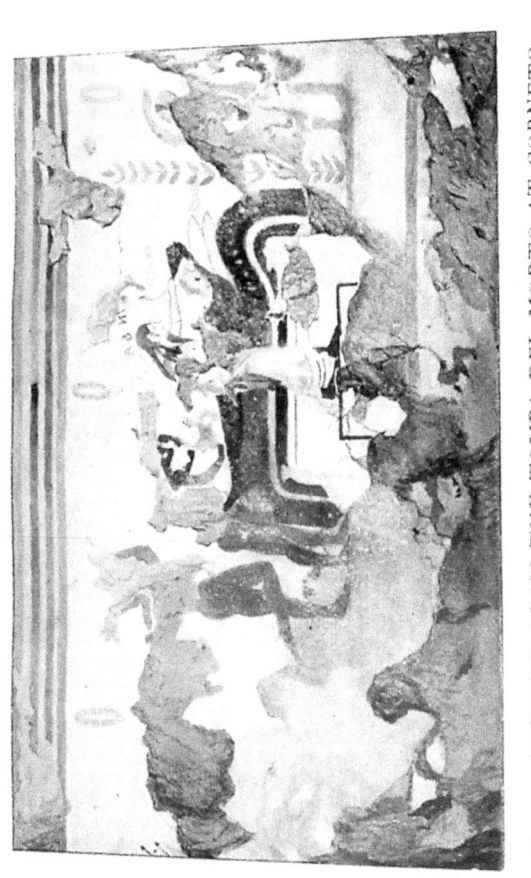

Fig. 9. PICTURE FROM THE TOMBA DEL MORTO AT CORNETO

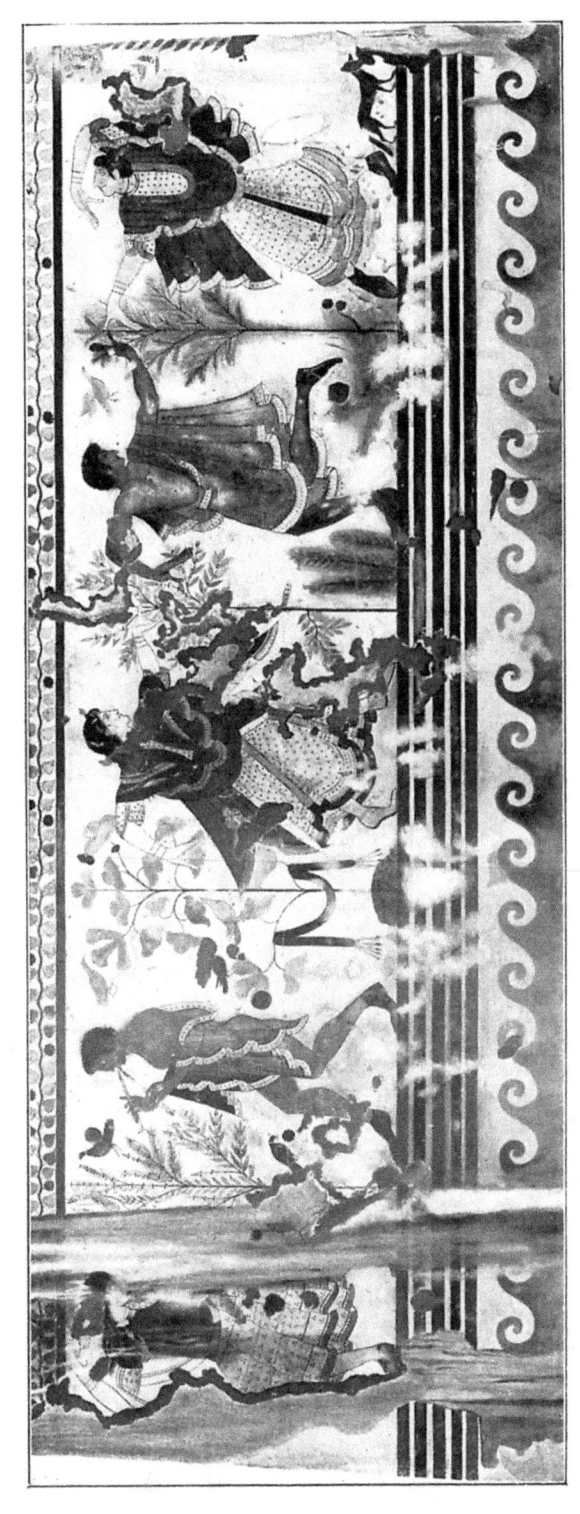

Fig. 10. PICTURE FROM THE TOMBA DEL TRICLINIO

totek contains several earlier, inferior facsimiles, made from the copies in the Museo Gregoriano and only touched up at Corneto by the painter Mariani;[1] and some more recent ones carefully executed on the spot (fig. 10). On each wall three female and two male dancers are seen among trees; fillets and singing-birds appear in the foliage. The male dancers play on lyre and flute; the dancing-girls have castanets and the foremost a strap or chaplet with bells over her shoulder. Similar chaplets with bells are often seen hanging on the walls in pictures representing the symposia in honour of the dead (see below), and bear witness to the childish predilection of the Etruscans for gipsy-like noise and merry-making. The most beautiful dancing-girl, however, in any Etruscan tomb is the already mentioned 'bella ballerina di Corneto', discovered on a wall in the Tomba Francesca Giustiniani. We give this figure, which has never been reproduced, after the facsimile in the Ny Carlsberg Glyptotek which arrived there shortly before the death of Carl Jacobsen and gave him one of the last pleasures in his life (fig. 11).

When I examined the original in the tomb at Corneto I made the following notes: the drapery (chiton), which is ornamented with a pattern of dotted rosettes, is distinctly preserved from the hips down to the elegant fluttering edge. Much of the middle part of the body has been destroyed; the fluttering ends of the red scarf across the shoulders are visible to right and left. The upper part of the body and the shoulders are also well preserved. The right arm is raised, and visible from shoulder to elbow; a faint outline of the left arm is also visible.[2] Of the head, the brow, the beginning of the nose, the ear, the green fluttering head-dress, the red hair with a loosened tress in front of the ear have been preserved. To the spectator the picture still conveys an impression of joy, of graceful movement, and of filmy fluttering draperies.

[1] Helbig's letters of June 21 and December 10, 1895.

[2] Thus the facsimile at this point gives more than I at any rate could see: on the other hand, less as far as brow and nose are concerned.

Here also we find Etruscan tradition continued on Roman soil, not only in the dancers of the festival processions, but in the tradition that Etruscan dancers, *ludii* or *ludiones*, were imported to Rome to dance at the great festivals. The Greeks compared the Roman reel to the Dionysiac ' cancan ', σίκιννις, while its Roman name is *tripudium* ; it was danced at every period of Roman history by the Salii, the ancient priesthood of the Roman war-god, on the chief festival of the god, March 19. According to Livy (vii. 2. 4–7) the earliest Roman poetry, the coarse Fescennines, originated in the text which accompanied the dance of the *ludiones*, and the fact that the dancers during the Fescennines daubed their faces with minium supports the theory of Etruscan influence, which also makes itself felt in the custom observed by the Roman triumphators, who in the earliest times daubed their whole bodies with minium. For we know that the Etruscans coated the images of their gods with minium at their festivals, and that the Romans gave the ancient terracotta statue of the Capitoline Jupiter a similar coat of ' war paint ' at the high festivals, a task which it fell to the censors to superintend.[1] The red minium was meant to heighten the natural red-brown hue of the men ; it produced an artificial virile complexion, just as white lead and chalk served to emphasize the pale feminine hue.[2]

The primitive nature of the verses connected with these dances is shown by the song of the Salii, the burden of which is the five times repeated ' triumpe ' (jump !) and the text of which runs : ' Help us, lares, let not the evil disease fall upon any more of us, Mars ! Be satisfied, cruel Mars ! Jump on to the threshold. Cease jumping. Help us, Mars ! ' At the triumphs also, ' carmina incondita ', as Livy tells us, were sung (iv. 20. 2), and we venture to think that Etruscan poetry was no better than this, and that the disappearance of the texts, which accompanied the dances, is

---

[1] Plutarch, *Aetia Romana* 98.
[2] Plautus, *Truculentus* 290, 294, *Mostellaria* 259 ff. In Greece also, women used white lead as paint: Lysias i. 14 and 17.

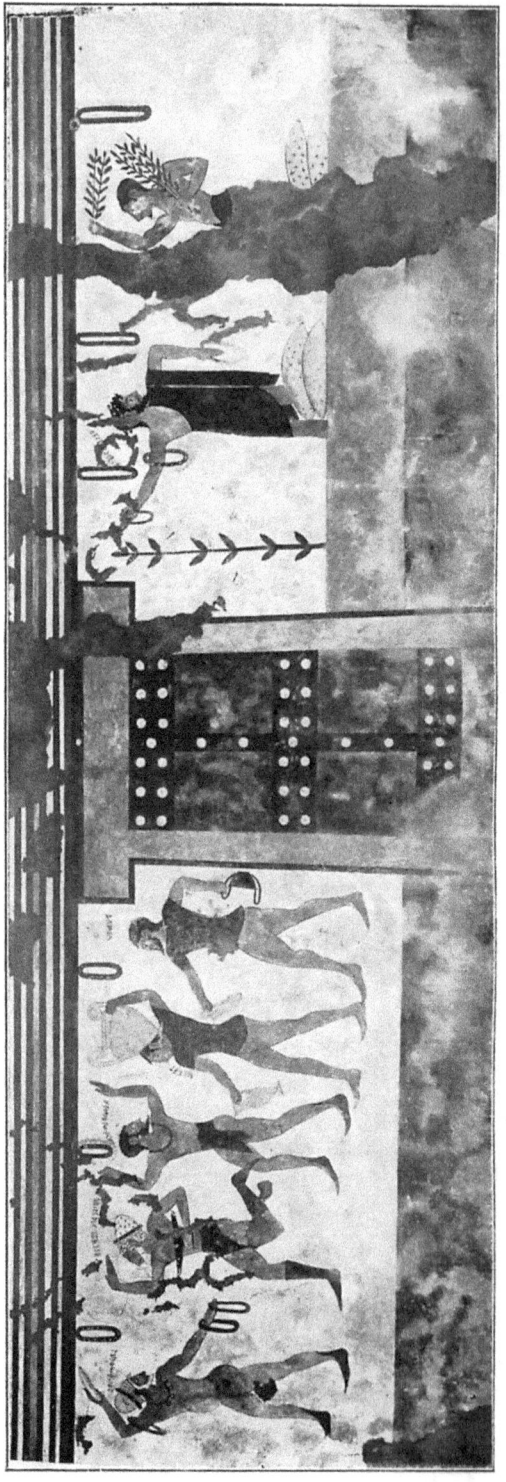

Fig. 12. RIGHT MAIN WALL IN THE TOMBA DELLE ISCRIZIONI

no great loss. Varro mentions tragedies in the Etruscan language, but they were undoubtedly versions of the Greek ones, even worse than those made for the Romans by Livius Andronicus. Apart from some religious and a little historical literature, and a number of recipes for the gathering of simples, capable of rousing the admiration of the Greeks for ' the descendants of the Tyrrhenians, the people skilled in medical lore ',[1] no tradition of any Etruscan intellectual life in writing or poetry has been handed down to posterity.

We pass on to the right main wall in the Tomba delle Iscrizioni (fig. 12) where dancers in a row with drinking-bowls in their hands alternate with servants carrying wine in large bowls. That the funeral dance was animated by free indulgence in wine is often exemplified in the tombs. In the Tomba delle Leonesse, named after the beasts of prey in the pediment, which are really hunting leopards, a red-brown lad to the right is dancing with a girl ; to the left is a woman with castanets, and in the centre, flanked by a flute-player and a lyre-player, stands the wine-bowl wreathed with fresh leaves (fig. 13), ' the wine-bowl filled with joy,' in Xenophanes' words. Evidently the Etruscans drank heavily to celebrate the memory of their dead, as Xenophon relates of another barbarian tribe, the Odrysians.[2] To the right of the false door of the same main wall in the Tomba delle Iscrizioni (fig. 12), a man in a loin-cloth with a laurel branch in each hand is greeting another man, who carries chaplets and rests one leg on the cushions of a couch. Laurel branches constantly recur in the reliefs of the Etruscan cinerary urns, where the death lament round the bier of the deceased is reproduced, and it seems probable that laurel branches were carried round the house and used for wall decoration in the house of the deceased on the funeral day, for the purpose of purification. This decoration of the walls, then, would be the subject of our picture, together with the other preparations

---

[1] Quotation from Aeschylus by Theophrastus (who endorses the opinion): *History of Plants* ix. 15. 1.
[2] *Hellenica* iii. 2. 5.

for the funeral, as shown by the paintings.[1] Perhaps it was a general custom of the Etruscans to decorate their walls on festival days with laurel branches, just as the Egyptians decorated theirs with lotus, and this would often account for all the foliage which appears in the backgrounds of the paintings alternating with suspended chaplets, even where the action—the death lament (fig. 9) or the symposium—takes place indoors. In other cases, however, as in the Tomba dei Tori (fig. 2) and in the Tomba del Triclinio (fig. 10), there is no doubt that real trees and open-air scenes are represented, but even there the chaplets are often seen hanging—on the wall. Again a proof of the want of clarity in Etruscan art ! Trees, however, in the background of scenes with figures are also found on South Italian vases of the same time, and thus seem to be a common Italic trait.

VI

CONTEMPORARY with the group of the Tomba degli Auguri and the Tomba delle Iscrizioni is the Tomba del Barone, discovered at Corneto in 1827 and named, as already mentioned, after Baron Kestner. After the paintings of this tomb Stackelberg executed a fine water-colour, and Thürmer a number of drawings, now in the University of Strasburg. The style—both in the shape of the heads and in the treatment of the draperies—is still Ionic, but the proportions are more slender, probably owing to Chian or Attic influence.

Composition and technique are both unique in the paintings of this tomb. We content ourselves with reproducing one main wall, the left (fig. 14), where a black horse with light grey hoofs, mane, and tail, is led by a man wearing red boots and a brown mantle lined with green. He is

[1] Cp. Tacitus, *Histor.* iv. 53, on the inauguration of the rebuilt Capitolium : ' spatium omne quod templo dicabatur evinctum vittis coronisque; ingressi milites, quis fausta nomina, *felicibus ramis.*'

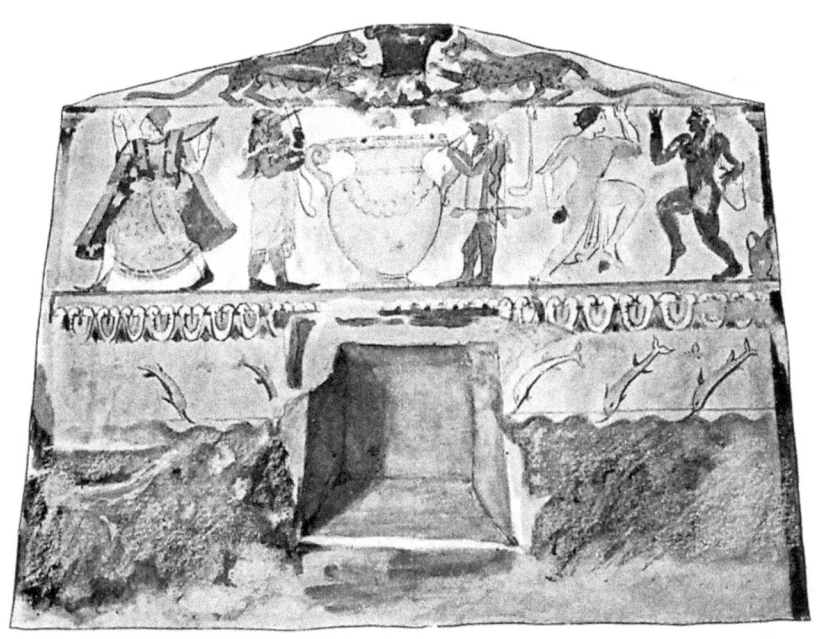

FIG. 13. BACK WALL IN THE TOMBA DELLE LEONESSE
After a drawing in the Helbig Museum

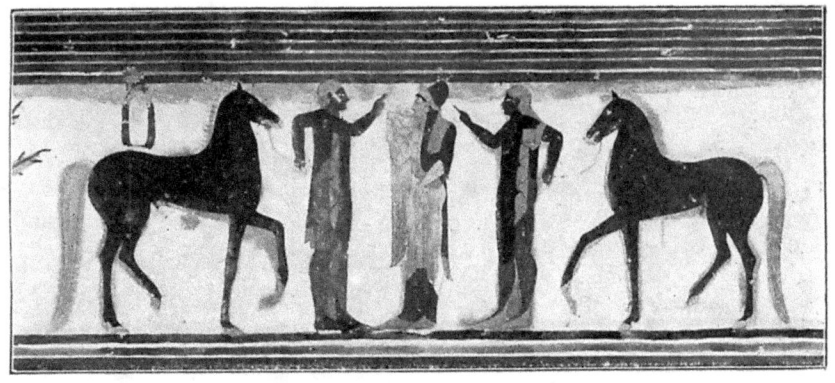

FIG. 14. LEFT MAIN WALL IN THE TOMBA DEL BARONE

speaking with one hand raised to a woman in a long grey chiton, a brown mantle lined with green, and a brown cap. Then comes a man with green boots leading a brown horse.

Similar quiet pictures are found on the other two walls of the tomb ; on the back wall a man is standing with his arm round a young flute-player's neck, and is greeted by a woman. The dress of the women is Etruscan; the subjects also are probably Etruscan—the preparations for the pompa and the dancing feast. But everything breathes coolness and calm, and we miss the usual jollity. The technique is equally remarkable. It is not the usual fresco painting : experiments have been made with size-paint, that is, an attempt at painting in distemper on the plaster stucco covering the walls. The attempt has failed ; the colour has run in large blotches.

These two characteristics of the artist of the Tomba del Barone are of great interest because the German archaeologist, Gustav Körte, has demonstrated the existence of marks made by Greek artisans on the walls of this tomb. It was not in Etruscan, but in Greek letters that the artist indicated the amount of his day's work, with a view to his wages. The explanation, then, seems to be the following : a Greek decorator was charged with the task of ornamenting the walls of the tomb, and he did it, as far as the dresses are concerned, according to local tradition ; but he experimented boldly with a new technical process, the success of which was prevented by the dampness of the rock-wall; and he composed his pictures with a grandeur of line and a tranquillity in execution which make one think of the pediment of a Greek temple. In the light of this it is easier to realize how much of the Etruscan temperament there really is in the other paintings, all Greek influence on style notwithstanding. It must be noted here that artisans' marks are the only written evidence left by the decorative painters of Etruria ; artists' signatures are unknown, whether in Greek or in Etruscan. The Etruscan nobles, like the Roman later, evidently employed Greek artists, but granted them no social position.

VII

IN the next period the predominant stylistic influence is
Attic. A whole group of tombs dates from about 500 B. C. :
they are thus contemporaneous with the severe red-figured
vase-paintings. Very Attic and, at the same time, like a
complete pictorial procession, representing everything which
took place at a great Etruscan funeral, is the Tomba delle
Bighe, previously mentioned and now published by Weege.
As the pictures in this tomb are clearer and more complete
than most Etruscan paintings, we will take some of them as
a starting-point for a closer examination of the facts of
Etruscan life.

There are two friezes on the three walls of the tomb : a
narrower and lighter above ; and a broader one below, in
which the figures are painted on a deep red ground ; the
height of the friezes is respectively 36 and 90 cm., and they
are separated by a broad, coloured band. The narrow frieze
with the dark figures on light ground still reminds one of the
black-figured Attic vases, whereas the lower purple frieze, in
which the skin of the men is reserved in a somewhat lighter
red, that of the women in white, recalls the red-figured vase-
paintings, all differences notwithstanding.

On the right-hand main wall (fig. 15), in the broad frieze,
men and women are dancing in honour of the dead among
laurel branches. There are the usual ecstasy and the familiar
animated gestures with the big fan-like hands, reminding one
of the figures in archaic Greek vase-painting and plastic art.[1]

Especially splendid is the female flute-player who turns
round as she dances, her light chiton and red cloak fluttering
about her ; she can almost compare with ' la bella ballerina '.
The dancing-women all wear the high Etruscan wreathed
cap, the so-called *tutulus*, which in the Tomba delle Iscrizioni
is also worn by a male dancer. We meet with it again in
Etruscan terracotta sculpture. The fashion is of Oriental

[1] Cp. Fr. Poulsen, *Delphi*, fig. 44.

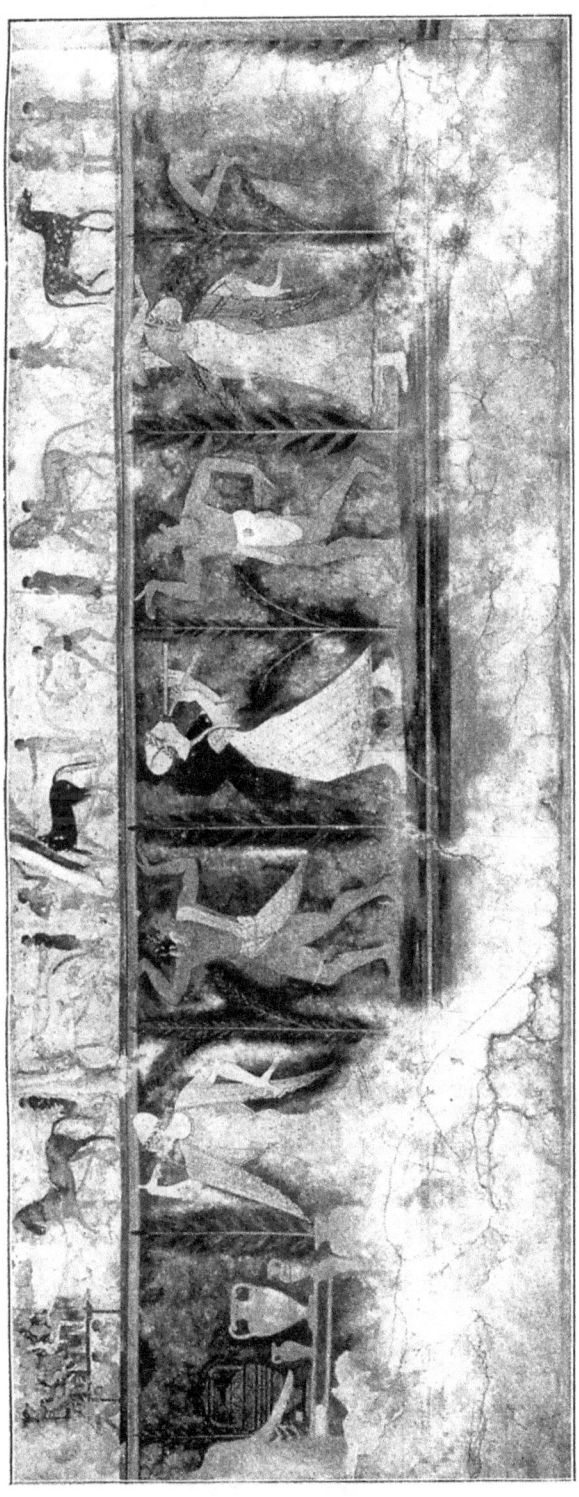

FIG. 15. RIGHT MAIN WALL IN THE TOMBA DELLE BIGHE

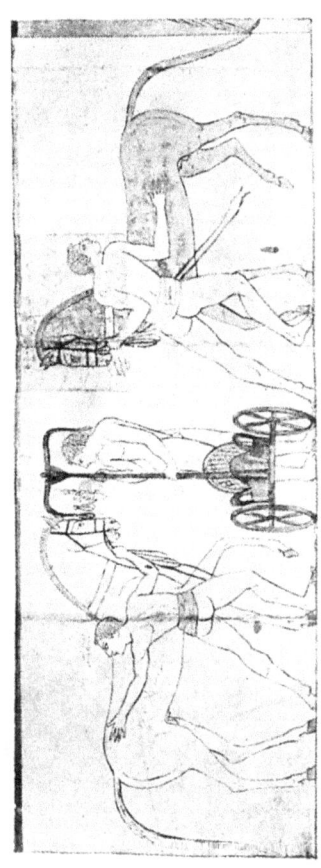

FIG. 17. PART OF THE SMALL FRIEZE IN THE
TOMBA DELLE BIGHE

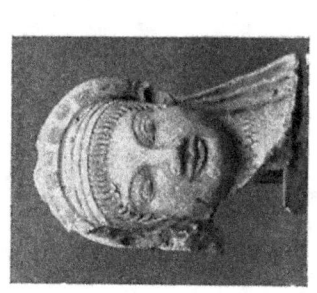

FIG. 16. ETRUSCAN TERRA-COTTA HEAD IN
THE NY CARLSBERG GLYPTOTEK

origin, and goes back, ultimately, to the pointed ' sugar-loaf hat ' of the Hittites. It probably reached Etruria by way of Cyprus, where it is frequently seen in reliefs of the seventh century B. C. In Etruria the pointed woollen cap became part of the national dress.[1] Rome of course adopted the headgear and preserved the Etruscan tradition in the priest-hoods ; a purple tutulus adorned the Roman Flaminicae, and certain secondary priests wore a tutulus down to the time of Tertullian.[2] In early Rome all women wore the tutulus, and under it a head-cloth such as is shown in Etruscan terracottas (fig. 16) ; this is clear from a description of a Roman mourning scene in Dionysius of Halicarnassus (xi. 39), where the women tear their many and various fillets and hair-ornaments off their heads.[3]

The dancing scene, in the painted frieze referred to above (fig. 15), ends at the sideboard on the left, which bears a number of metal bowls : a cup-bearer, partially obliterated in the original, is just putting down a vessel. The wine to inspire the dancers is ready.

In the narrow frieze—the most beautiful and most care-fully executed of those in the tomb, but very badly copied in the facsimile of the Glyptotek—we see the preparations for a chariot race. The horses are being led out and harnessed to the chariot. We reproduce, after Stackelberg's drawing, the most interesting part of the frieze (fig. 17), in which three young men are busy harnessing two horses to the light, two-wheeled chariot, the Biga. The chariot is represented in foreshortening, and the shaft is lifted up by a naked boy. The young men have each one foot strongly foreshortened.

[1] Daremberg-Saglio, s. v. Tutulus. Fr. Poulsen, Der Orient und die früh-griech. Kunst, p. 97, fig. 99, and p. 107. Martha, L'art étrusque, p. 306, fig. 206 (Cyprus). Antike Denkmäler iii, pl. 1.

[2] In the same manner the Roman priests used flint knives in their cult, and their razors had to be of copper, and, as late as Roman imperial times, they used black vessels (nigrum catinum), corresponding to the Etrus-can bucchero vases, at sacrifices. Livy i. 24. 9 : Juvenal vi. 343. Cp. Müller-Deecke, Die Etrusker ii. p. 275.

[3] The Latin name of the head-cloth is struppus, and from that a festival at Falerii, struppearia, derived its name. It comes from Ionia, and is mentioned in the poems of Sappho (χειρόμακτρον).

We find here the same experimentation with this new and difficult problem, as in the Greek vase-paintings of about 500 B. C., in the vases of Euthymides and Euphronius. The horse to the right is blue, that to the left grey, both have red hoofs and red harness, and two youths, with a sort of shawl round their loins, are busily engaged with them, striking them on the flanks to get them into place. These two excellent figures are quite misdrawn and misconstrued in the Ny Carlsberg facsimile, the draughtsman not having realized that they are seen from behind.

We have, therefore, preparations for a chariot race ; in a wall-painting in the Tomba del Morente at Corneto we have a still earlier phase represented, the lassoing of the horse which is to be harnessed (fig. 18) ; here the horse is red, with blue mane and tail. The disposition of the colours is no more naturalistic in Etruscan wall-painting than in the pediments of Greek temples : in applying the colours, the painter's object was purely decorative.

After the preparations comes the ceremonial parade of the racing chariots past the stands ; three chariots are seen in a row (fig. 15): the first has not yet begun to move, the horses are pawing the ground impatiently, and the groom is standing at their heads trying to pacify them ; the second chariot has already started, and the team of the third chariot is going a little faster, a fine crescendo which reminds one of good Greek art rather than of Etruscan. To the left are the stands for the spectators, which are continued on the back wall ; similar stands are seen in the corner where back wall and left main wall adjoin. We give, after Stackelberg's drawing, the two parts from the first-mentioned corner (fig. 19). On elevated platforms, bounded above by lines evidently meant to indicate curtains which might be drawn before the 'box' against sun or heavy showers, men and women are seated and show their absorption in the games by their eager gestures. The foremost woman to the right actually greets the procession of chariots with her raised hand. She is a matron wearing a shawl (epiblema) over the

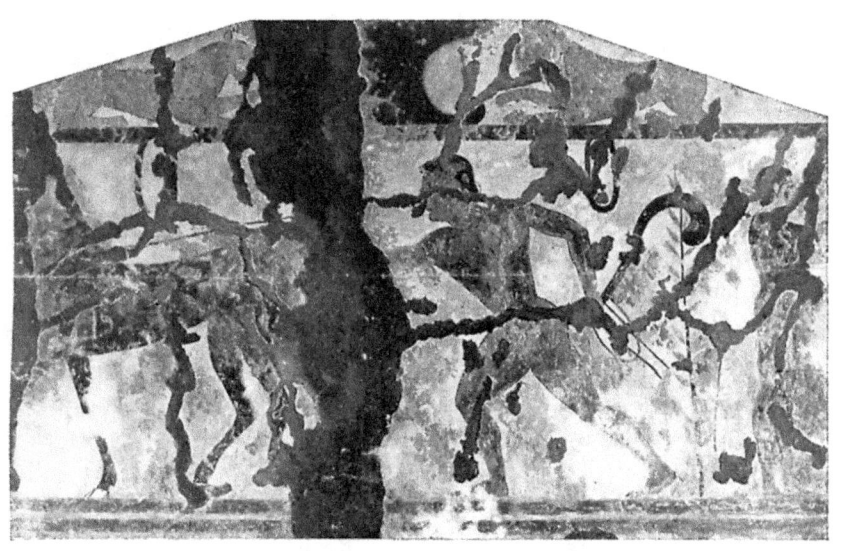

FIG. 18. WALL-PAINTING FROM THE TOMBA DEL MORENTE
THE LASSOING OF THE HORSE

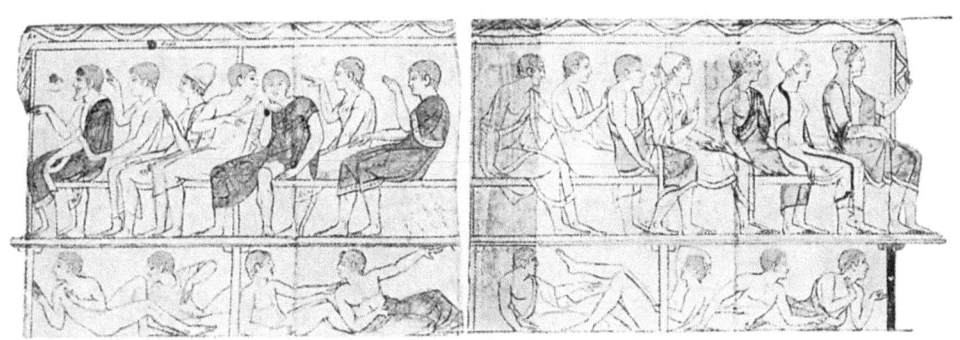

FIG. 19. PART OF THE SMALL FRIEZE IN THE TOMBA DELLE BIGHE
After Arch. Jahrb. 1916

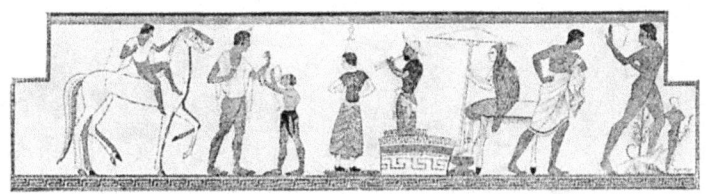

FIG. 20. PART OF THE TOMBA DELLA SCIMMIA
AT CHIUSI

arms, and the back of her head, and under that a tutulus. Next to her sits a young girl with a tutulus, noble in bearing and gesture like a young goddess. Then follows a varied company of youths, women, and a bearded man. The young man, who is represented partly frontal with his chin resting on his hand and the head and left leg frontal, is of special interest. The problem of foreshortening has been very neatly solved. Under the wooden floor of the stands the common folk are disporting themselves, some of them engrossed in anything but the games.

In order to understand the significance of this representation one has to realize that such detailed pictures of spectators at athletic games are unknown in Greek art. The nearest parallel is the assembly of the gods, the Olympian spectators, in the frieze of the Treasury of the Siphnians at Delphi,[1] and in the Parthenon frieze, between which the Tomba delle Bighe chronologically occupies an intermediate position, about twenty-five years later than the former, and about fifty years earlier than the latter. At the same time we learn that female spectators were also present; this was not so at the Olympic games, but seems to have been a common Italic custom. The stands, too, appear typically Italic; on such ἴκρια the spectators were seated at those athletic games and contests which in earlier times, according to Vitruvius (v. 1), were held in the market-places of Italian towns. Amphitheatres were not known till the first century B.C., but if one imagines these market-places on festival days with such wooden stands built up on all four sides, and these stands curved round at the corners in order that the spectators might see better, one can understand how the shape of the amphitheatre originated.[2]

Within the sphere of Etruscan painting also, this is the only large representation of an audience. Elsewhere the artist limited himself to the individual figure as representative of the spectators; thus in the Tomba della Scimmia (the

[1] Fr. Poulsen, *Delphi*, fig. 44.
[2] Cp. Daremberg-Saglio and Pauly-Wissowa, *s. v. Amphitheatrum*.

Monkey Tomb) at Chiusi, the only spectator is a lady dressed in black and sheltered by a sunshade ; she is seated on a high chair without a back (diphros), her feet on a footstool (fig. 20). The tomb was discovered in 1846 by François. The pictures are executed in a thin colour, probably a sort of water-colour, applied directly to the stone without an intermediate layer of stucco ; a similar technique is employed in the other and larger tomb at Chiusi, the Tomba Casuccini. The four walls are decorated with scenes from the race-course and the palaestra. Behind the lady on the wall which is reproduced, we see two men in rapid motion and with ample gestures probably intended to render the bustle and hurry at the funeral, which is also represented, as we have seen, by one of the figures in the Augur tomb (cp. fig. 4). The sunshade carried by the ' widow ' was an Oriental fashion, but in the fifth century B.C. the women of Greece had adopted it, as is shown by the *Knights* of Aristophanes (l. 1348 σκιάδειον). To the left the usual flute-player is standing, and the round dais in front of him is not an altar, but, as Milani was the first to point out, the small table on which prizes were placed.[1] Next comes a girl with a censer on her head. She is generally taken to be a female juggler, but carrying a tall object on one's head is still a common practice with the women of the South, and censers (thymiateria), as we learn from Dionysius of Halicarnassus, were always carried at the ' pompae ' in early Rome ; at the high festivals they were placed in front of the Roman doorways.[2] They were sometimes of costly material.[3] But our woman seems to be standing on a platform, and the near presence of the flute-player, and the turning of her body and position of her arms, seem to indicate some difficult dance performed with the big object borne on her head in a small, limited space ; hence a kind of old Etruscan dervish-dance of which we have no other knowledge. The two figures next to her are a big and a small man who are cooling their bleeding noses

[1] *Museo archeol. di Firenze*, p. 303.   [3] Cicero, *In Verrem* iv. 46. See
[2] Livy xxix. 14. 13.   also Karl Wigand, *Thymiateria*.

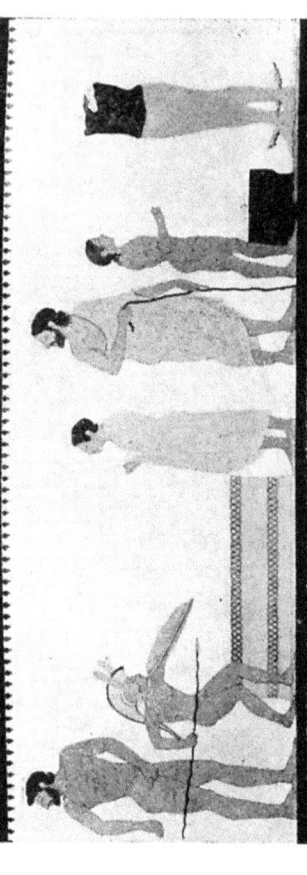

FIG. 22

PART OF THE SMALL FRIEZE IN THE TOMBA DELLE BIGHE

After Arch. Jahrb. 1916

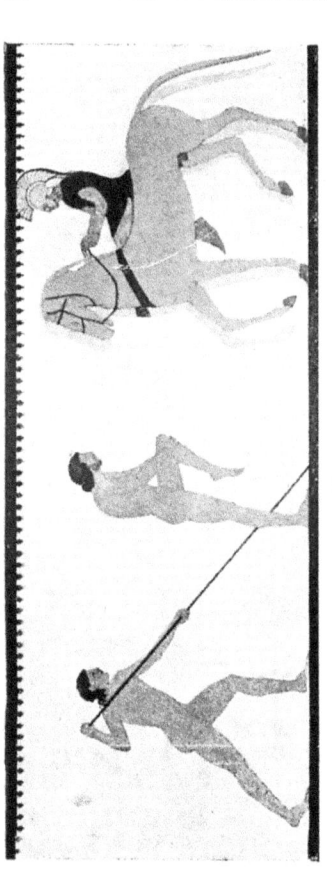

FIG. 21

PART OF THE SMALL FRIEZE IN THE TOMBA DELLE BIGHE

After Arch. Jahrb. 1916

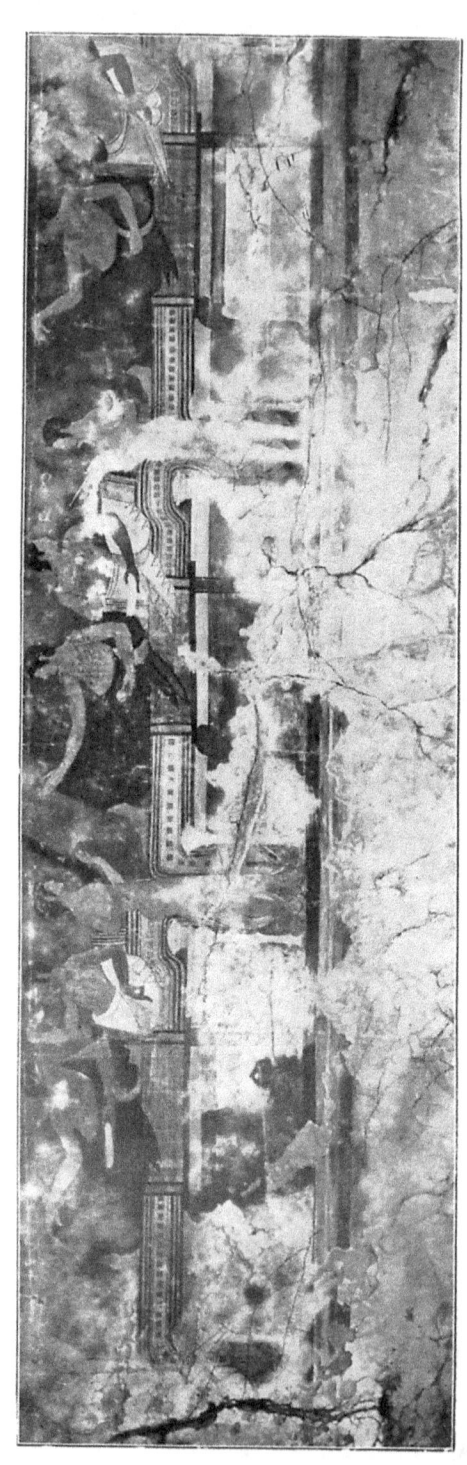

FIG. 23. SYMPOSIUM IN THE TOMBA DELLE BIGHE

with sponges : the artist gives the atmosphere of the scene after the fight. On one of the other walls in this tomb the boxers are ready for action, raising their cestus-bound fists against each other, one hand closed for attack, the other open for defence, as frequently described in the ancient authors.[1] Cicero tells us that boxers sighed and groaned, in order to increase the force of the blow.[2] These cestus fights must have been terrible. The guard, nowadays less, was then more important than the blow, for it was too dangerous to take the risk of being hit by one's opponent when attacking him, even if one was confident that one's own blow would be the harder ; one had to play for an opening, at the same time guarding against the single blow which was sufficient to knock a man out. Finally, on the extreme left of the picture (fig. 20) we meet with a scene which is repeated in another picture in the same tomb, as well as in the Tomba del Triclinio : a rider seated sideways and at the same time leading another horse. The race with a led horse was an Oriental custom, and appears for the first time on the Phoenician metal bowls of the eighth and seventh centuries B.C. This seat, sideways on the horse, is of Scythian origin, and in Greek art usually characterizes the Amazons. The Etruscans, with their passion for difficult games, evidently combined the two in order to make the races as exciting as possible.

In the small frieze on the back wall of the Tomba delle Bighe we find a rider with a led horse, dressed in tunic and helmet, and seated astride ; we reproduce part of it after Stackelberg's water-colour (fig. 21). To the left of him we see a naked man standing on one leg and nursing his raised left leg. It was formerly conjectured that he was playing leap-frog with the young man planting the jumping-pole in the ground behind him, but it is not usual to play leap-frog on one leg, and Weege has pointed out the same position in athletic scenes on Greek vases and supposes it to be a kind of preparatory exercise. His supposition is correct : any

[1] For instance in Apollonius Rhodius, *Argonautica* ii. 68.

[2] Cicero, *Tusculanae disputationes* ii. 56.

modern acrobat would recognize it as one of his exercises ; the contraction of the muscles by nursing right and left knee in turn. Acrobats practise this exercise when travelling, to keep themselves fit when they are unable to train.

VIII

WE will not dwell on all the forms of wrestling contests and boxing matches which appear in the small frieze of the Bighe tomb, but only describe a part of the left main wall, which presents an important and difficult problem (fig. 22). To the left of a young man in a himation (not reproduced) we see the lower part of a statue of a deity, who would seem, from the faint traces in Stackelberg's water-colour, to have wings on his ankles. If so, it is Hermes, the protector of the palaestra, and the black object in front of him is a small altar. On the other side of the altar a boy, accompanied by one of the caretakers of the palaestra, clad in a blue mantle and carrying a knotted stick, is standing with his hand raised. This usually indicates the adorer praying to the divinity for victory in the contest. An absolutely Greek palaestra interior! We have now escaped from the sphere of the customary rude games held at the Etruscan funerals, and the question arises whether the Etruscan knew real palaestra life of the Greek type or not. In the Oscan towns of Lucania and Campania the youths were devoted to Greek sports, and Weege is therefore inclined, in view especially of this picture, to believe the same of the nobles of Etruria at the height of their glory in the sixth and fifth centuries B.C. But this is a dangerous inference. Wherever else we meet with Etruscan athletic types they are rough and lumbering of build and evidently professionals. In the Tomba delle Bighe a Greek artist has been at work ; this was already admitted by Stackelberg and Kestner, and the same view is held in our own times. Although the artist has complied with the demands of his patron more fully than the Greek artist in the Tomba del Barone, who only troubled himself to do so as far as dress was concerned, but for the rest painted entirely in the spirit of his native country, Greek influence, nevertheless, has penetrated everywhere. It is seen, for instance, in the incongruities of the picture : the spectators in the corners, suggesting actual athletic games ; then this interior from a Greek palaestra, which *might* be interpreted, however, as part of a public contest ; next comes the prize table, as in the Tomba della Scimmia, but on both sides himation-clad boys are seen, loitering like typical figures of the everyday life of the palaestra, who have absolutely nothing to do with the concentrated excitement of the sports in the arena. To the left of the low table we see a little armed dancer, with helmet, shield, and spear, in Greek nudity, not fully dressed like the gladiator in the Tomba della Scimmia ; his lance is bent zigzag-wise, apparently an Etruscan peculiarity. With the Greeks also, the armed dance—the pyrrhiche—formed part of the sepulchral festival, especially in Cyprus and Crete, where it was called prylis ;[1] and the custom may very well have been adopted by the Etruscans.

IX

SIMILAR incongruities, due to Greek artists, or at any rate Greek art, having set a Greek stamp on the wall-painting of Etruria, meet us in the representations of *symposia*. Again we can take the Bighe tomb as our starting-point (fig. 23).[2] Three festive couches are seen with two young men on each.

[1] Aristotle, *fragm.* 519 R. Scholia to Homer's *Iliad* xxiii. 130. A similar dancer or armed runner appears in the Tomba Casuccini at Chiusi ; both remind us in posture of the Tübingen armed runner (Bulle, *Der schöne Mensch*, pl. 89).

[2] The large frieze with dancing scenes on the left main wall was already badly damaged in 1827. A copy of it, now in the Vatican, is mere fiction, and has unfortunately served as basis for the large facsimile in the Glyptotek. On the other hand, its damaged state is correctly represented in the small drawing of the tomb in the Glyptotek.

The youths are naked to the waist, and have sumptuous gold necklaces, red or blue mantles, and chaplets on their heads. Some of them hold flat drinking-bowls, some eggs, and others have branches in their hands—all this, however, we only learn from the old copies : they are reclining on metal couches, whereas the tables in front of them are wooden, as is clearly proved by the colours employed. We may wonder that the couches are of metal, for according to the literary tradition the first metal couches came to Rome as late as 187 B.C. Nevertheless, ivory and golden couches are already mentioned by Plautus ; this may, however, be due to the Greek text on which he based his comedy (*Stichus* 377). The Etruscans, at any rate, knew bronze couches at least three hundred years earlier, and this is corroborated by the find of an actual bronze banqueting-couch in a tomb at Corneto.[1] The couches are covered with many-coloured woven or embroidered bolsters and cushions ; these also are mentioned in the Roman comedies as ornaments of couches.[2] Ducks appear beneath the couches, and the guests are attended by three naked lads : a flute-player, a boy holding a branch, and another with a ladle, which are wrongly reproduced in the Ny Carlsberg facsimile as a staff.

The symposium has begun, the tables having been cleared. Only young beardless men are seen feasting together, and nothing informs us who they are or why they are drinking. All that is certain is the luxury and pomp which seem to have characterized Etruscan houses and which are especially manifest in the jingling necklaces and the material and appointment of the festive couch.

New problems arise with the large symposium scene in the Tomba dei Leopardi at Corneto, which was discovered in 1875 and has now been described in an exemplary manner

[1] Blümner, *Römische Privataltertümer*, p. 118.

[2] On Etruscan cinerary urns and terracotta sarcophagi the covers are as a rule strongly scalloped. These are presumably the *tonsilia tappetia* referred to by Plautus (*Pseudolus* 145 ff.). They usually came from Alexandria and were decorated with pictures of wild beasts, whereas the bed coverlets proper came from Campania.

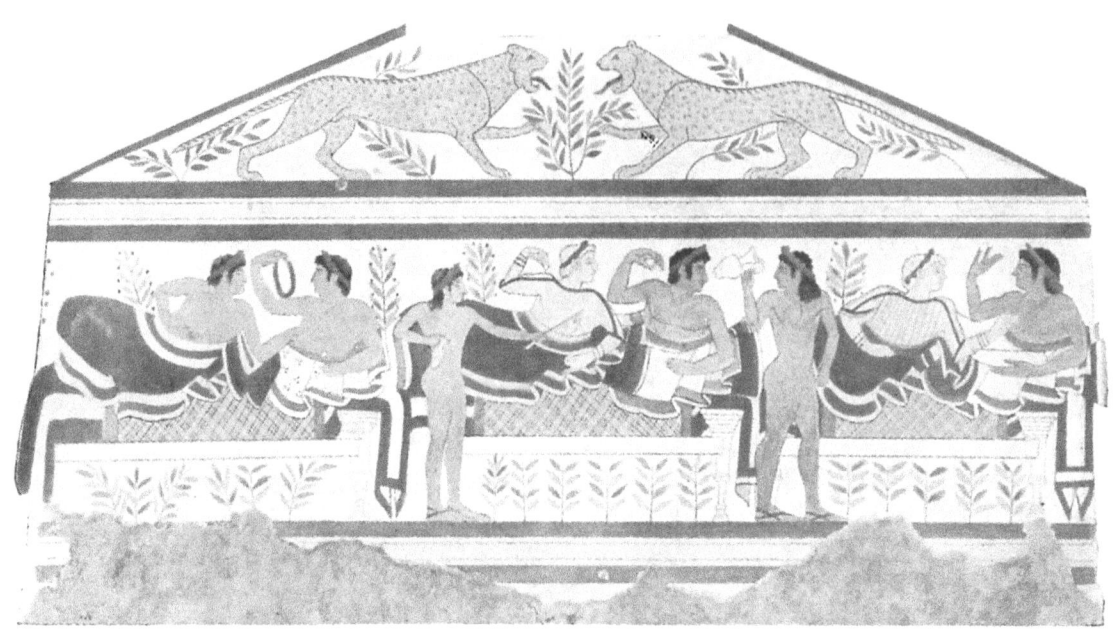

FIG. 24

BACK WALL IN THE TOMBA DEI LEOPARDI

After Arch. Jahrb. 1916, pl. 9

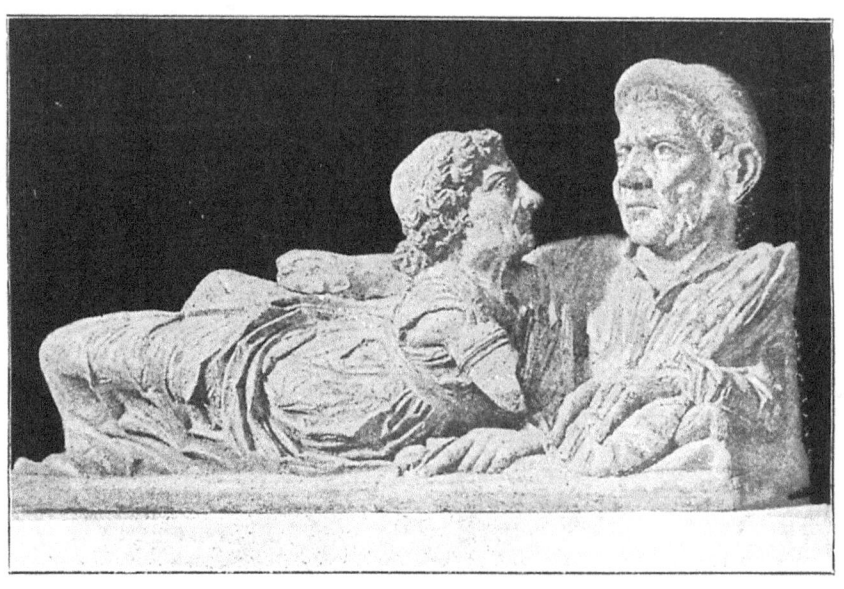

FIG. 25

MARRIED COUPLE ON AN ETRUSCAN CINERARY URN

by Weege in the article mentioned above. The pictures are among the best preserved in the whole of Etruria, and date from about the same time as the Bighe tomb, about 500 B.C. The tomb takes its name from the two almost life-sized leopards in the pediment (fig. 24). They have been neatly proved by Weege to be hunting leopards. As early as the days of ancient Egypt leopards were trained for hunting purposes, and hunting leopards appear in Greek vase-paintings and Etruscan wall-paintings, for instance, in the earlier tombs such as the Tomba delle Leonesse and the Tomba del Triclinio, where the animal lies beneath a couch. In the Middle Ages the hunting leopard was still trained in the East, and is therefore depicted in the paintings of the Renaissance—for instance in the pictures of Gentile da Fabriano and Benozzo Gozzoli—as seated on the cruppers of the horses behind the Magi or their servants.[1] In modern India leopards are still trained to hunt.

Beneath the two long-bodied hunting leopards we see the main picture of the back wall (fig. 24) representing a symposium. On the couch to the left two youths are reclining, on each of the two others a youth and a young girl.[2] The young men are attired in mantles, the girls in chitons and mantles ; all wear garlands. In their hands they hold either chaplets, drinking-bowls, or round objects usually supposed to be eggs. Similar ' eggs ' appear in numerous Etruscan banqueting-scenes : in the Tombe del Triclinio, del Letto funebre, della Pulcella, degli Scudi, &c., and as egg-shells are frequently found in the tombs at Corneto, and eggs must therefore have been offered to the dead [3]—as the most nourishing of foods, and one which stimulates in particular

[1] These cheetahs were brought alive to Italy, if not actually used for hunting by the princes of the Renaissance. For among Pisanello's drawings in the Codex Vallardi in the Louvre is a fine study of one of these animals from the life ; it wears a collar round its neck, showing that it was led on a leash.

I owe this reference to Mr. G. F. Hill.

[2] Dennis and Stryk are mistaken in speaking of a youth and a girl on the left couch ; the error is due to the damaged condition of the colouring.

[3] Cp. Juvenal, *Satires* v. 82, where eggs are referred to as a common course at funerals.

the procreative force—it is not improbable that the old interpretation is the correct one.   Weege supposes them to be ballot-balls used to decide who should be the master of the symposium (symposiarch), but this was usually decided by throwing dice.   A third conceivable interpretation, which I think might be acceptable in certain cases where a man and a woman hand each other these round objects, is that they are rings.   In Plautus's *Asinaria* (778) it is spoken of as typical of two young lovers reclining on one couch at the symposium that one of them gives the other his or her ring to look at.

Beneath and above the banqueting-couch we find the previously noted laurel branches—not laurel trees as Weege calls them—the familiar adornment of the walls.   The guests are served by two naked pages : one of these, who holds a jug, beckons to the other, who holds a small jug and a strainer, to make haste.   How necessary it was to strain the wine is seen from the description of the elder Cato.   The Latin word for cleaning the wine-jars of the grape-skins deposited by the wine is *deacinare*.[1]

X

THIS wall-painting is apparently a faithful copy of a Greek painted representation of a symposium with hetaerae, and this is also Weege's view of the scene.   In his opinion, those who take part in the drinking bouts of the young men are not married or respectable women, but hetaerae.   It seems to me that such a representation in a *tomb* would argue a complete dissolution of family relations in ancient Etruria, whether we choose to interpret the pictures as scenes from life, or as an expression of the wish that the next life might take the form of nothing more or less than a revel with hetaerae.   Weege maintains, further, that hetaerae reclined at table, whereas wives sat with their husbands : but this is

[1] Cato, *De re rustica* 26.   In the Greek pictures of symposia also the slave boy carries a strainer, ἠθμός.

contrary to the express literary tradition, according to which the Greeks were shocked because the Etruscan women reclined at table with men ' under the same coverlet '. The earliest authority for this statement is Aristotle [1] and, according to this and other accounts of the fourth century B.C., the free intercourse between men and women gave rise to much immorality, the women abandoning themselves to the strange men with whom they reclined.[2] It would have been absurd for the Greeks to take offence at this if it did not apply to free-born women of good family, but only to hetaerae, who in Hellas did exactly the same. How things were with the Greeks in this respect is made sufficiently clear by a passage in the orator Isaeus [3]: ' No one would dare to serenade married women, and neither do the married women attend banquets with their husbands, nor do they consider it proper to partake of meals with strangers, especially chance acquaintances.'

With this severe Athenian custom we must compare these scandalized Greek outbursts, and, at the same time, we must remember that in the fourth century B.C. Etruscan civilization and morals were already on the decline, so that an original latitude, which in the beginning of the fifth century was natural and did not affect the morals of domestic life, may at this time have been abused. Incidentally, we are able to ascertain the degree of exaggeration in another Greek account of the same time concerning the luxuriousness of the Etruscans [4]: ' They reclined on flowered cushions drinking out of sumptuous silver bowls and attended by servants in costly dresses, *sometimes by naked women*.' In the Etruscan paintings there are numerous naked pages in attendance, just as in the Greek symposium pictures, but not a single naked handmaid. As to the question whether respectable women reclined or

---

[1] Athenaeus i. 23 d. On the Etruscan custom of reclining at table, like the Greeks, and unlike the men of the Homeric age and later the Macedonians, who sat, see Athenaeus i. 17 f, 18 a.

[2] Athenaeus xii. 517 d. Cp. Dionys. Halic. ix. 16.

[3] Isaeus iii. 14.

[4] Athenaeus iv. 153 d. (= Timaeus, *fragm*. 18 in Müller, *Fragmenta histor. Graecorum*).

sat at table, invariable rules did not exist in Etruria any more than they existed in ancient Rome, where we know that Jupiter alone reclined at the lectisternia (the sacred banquets given by the state) whereas Juno and Minerva sat ; furthermore, in the last century of the republic, respectable women sat with the men at banquets, while brides reclined.[1] The practice of brides reclining can hardly, however, be accounted for except as a case of adherence to an ancient and honourable custom which was superseded by later and severer notions.

Etruscan works of art, however, give sufficient information to confute the whole of Weege's hetaera theory. Man and woman are often seen reclining together on Etruscan sarcophagi and cinerary urns, and on the face of it it would seem improbable that a man would have himself pictured on his sarcophagus with a hetaera. Dr. S. P. Cortsen kindly informs me that this view is confirmed by the fact that two of these cinerary urns with a pair of figures on the lid have an inscription in which the word *tusurthi* or *tusurthir* occurs—one of the few Etruscan words the signification of which is certain : it means 'spouses'.[2] And if we look at the type of womanhood represented in several of the recumbent couples on the later urns, when realism prevails in Etruscan portrait sculpture, the appellation hetaera becomes as preposterous as that of matrons is certain (fig. 25).[3]

But proof is furnished by the tomb-paintings themselves. In the Tomba degli Scudi at Corneto, discovered in 1870, and, to judge by the style, dating from the end of the fifth century B.C., the wife (as might be expected) is pictured sitting with her husband, who is reclining on the couch with

---

[1] Friedländer, *Sittengeschichte Roms* i. 472, 478, 493 f.

[2] *Corpus inscriptionum Etruscarum*, 3858, 3860.

[3] The Etruscan character for immorality is chiefly due to Theopompus (*fragm.* 222 in Müller, *Fragm. hist. Graec.* i. p. 315), but he gives similar descriptions of the Thessalians, and seems to have specialized in *chroniques scandaleuses*. Of equal value is his information that the Sybarites loved the Etruscans because of their luxuriousness (Athenaeus xii. 519 b). It is regrettable that Theophrastus' work on the Etruscans is lost ; it would have provided information of quite a different character. (Cp. the Scholia to Pindar, *Pythia* ii. 3.)

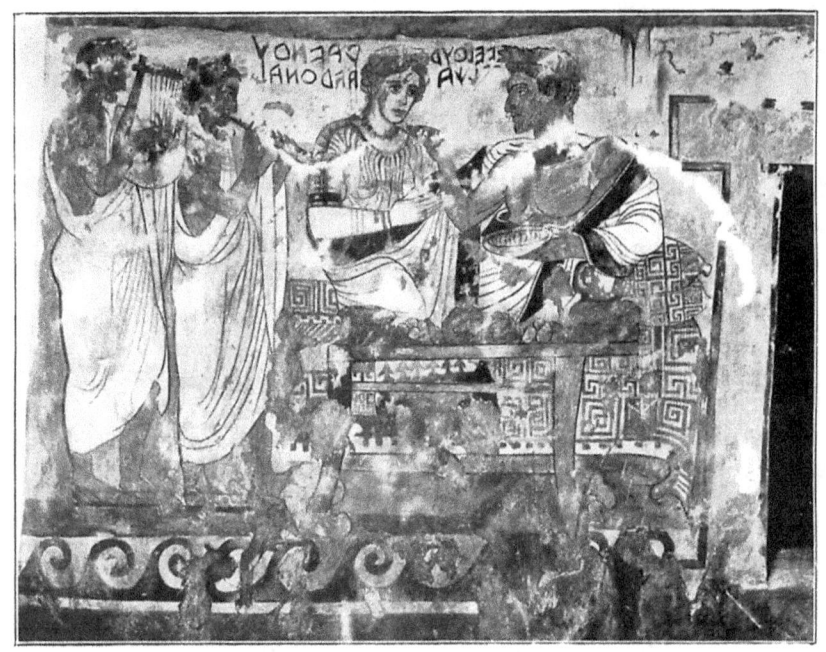

FIG. 26. PICTURE FROM THE TOMBA DEGLI SCUDI AT CORNETO

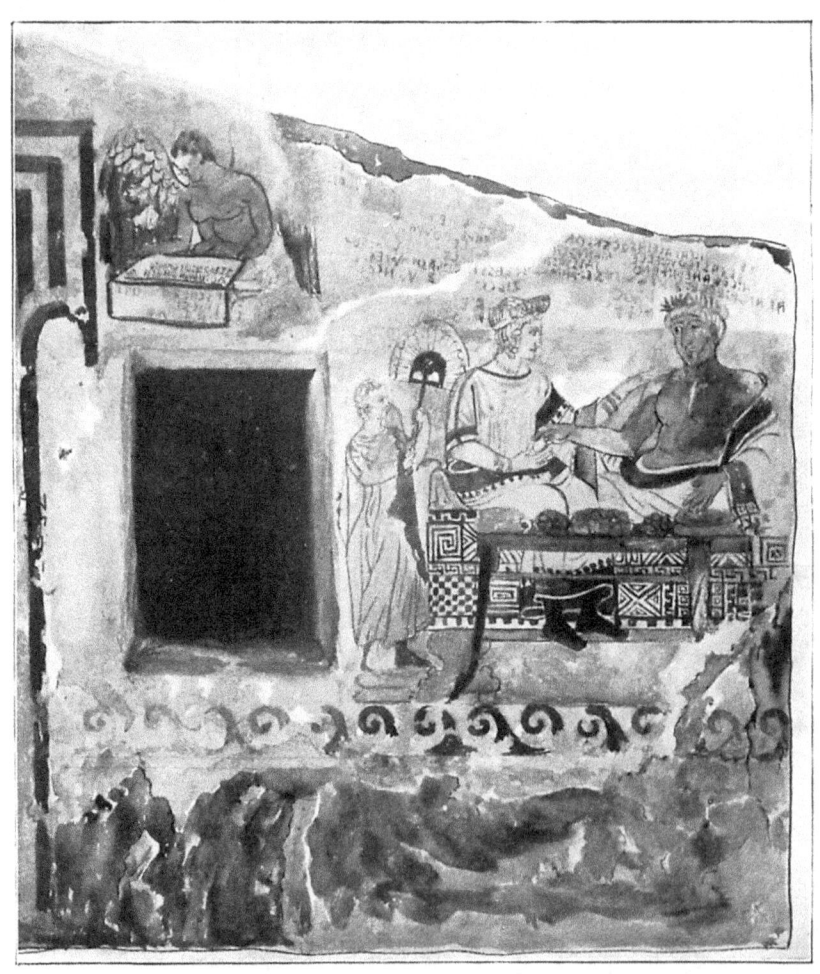

FIG. 27. PICTURE FROM THE TOMBA DEGLI SCUDI
After a coloured drawing in the Helbig Museum

a drinking-bowl in his left hand, his right resting on the woman's shoulder (fig. 26). According to the inscription the man's name is *Velthur Velcha*, that of the woman *Ravnthu Aprthnai* (the family name is in the nominative and is a woman's name, the Latin *Abortennia* ; so the family of the mother was the more distinguished). The figure and the diadem of the woman recall those of the Hera Borghese and determine the date of the tomb. On the table in front of the couch are a bowl, a cake (*pyramis*), and a heap of fruits : or they may be the ' ball-cakes ' (*spirae* or *spaeritae*) referred to by Cato (*De agricultura* 82). At the foot of the couch a lyre-player and a flute-player accompany the meal with music, recalling a statement of Cicero's [1] that at banquets in early Rome the sound of stringed instruments and flutes was deemed indispensable. On the whole, it might perhaps be as well to abandon all theories of the austere morals of early Rome. The patrician families of the first centuries of the republic undoubtedly lived a life which in pomp and luxury vied with the life of the nobility of the Etruscan towns. Again, in the painting on the back wall of this tomb, where the recumbent man is a priest (*cechaneri*), the wife is seated with her husband (fig. 27). As to the priest-hood, it must be borne in mind that the priestly office was hereditary in the Etruscan noble families. The statue of Juno at Veii, for instance, might only be touched by a priest of a certain family.[2] It was especially the art of divination, however, which was reserved for the noblemen and their wives.[3] Even when the Romans had conquered Etruria they continued to support the efforts of the Etruscans to confine initiation into the art of divination to the nobility. Even Cicero, in his book on the ideal State, maintains that omens and presages must be submitted to haruspices, and the nobles of Etruria must teach the ' disciplina '.

In the pictures of the Scudi tomb the wife, as we have

[1] *De oratore* iii. 197.
[2] Livy v. 22. 5.
[3] The most famous of all the Etrus- can women versed in divination is the wise but guileful Tanaquil, who played a political part in Rome : Livy i. 34.

seen, *is sitting*. But in the Tomba dei Vasi Dipinti, besides
a man and a woman, two children are present at the symposium, which would be inconceivable in a hetaera picture ; and
in a picture in the front chamber of the Tomba dell' Orco at
Corneto, discovered in 1868 and dating from the same period
as the Scudi tomb, there are traces of a man and a woman
reclining together, and the inscription informs us that the
woman is a free-born woman named Velia—the family name
has unfortunately been destroyed—and that she is married
to Arnth Velchas, a descendant of one of the noblest families
in Etruria (fig. 28). With this, then, the last and final proof
of the untenability of the hetaera theory has been adduced :
this woman, whose head is one of the most beautiful in the
sepulchral chambers of Etruria (fig. 29), reclines with her
husband on the couch in the picture in the tomb, even as she
was buried with him in the tomb itself. A failure to appreciate
this fact would imply a complete denial of Etruscan family
feeling and pride of race.

The dancing women, on the other hand, for instance, the
woman in the Tomba delle Leonesse already cited above,
and another, still more wanton, who in the Tomba degli
Bacchanti foots it with a fat dancer, must be interpreted
as hetaerae. They illustrate the phrase of Plautus : ' pro-
stibile est tandem ? stantem stanti savium dare amicum
amicae ? ' To the same category of hired dancers belongs
the man to the left of the one who is dancing with inverted
cithara.[1]

Generally speaking, what has made doubt or error possible
in the matter is the fact that the pictures, as we have already
said, in form suggest Greek pictures of hetaerae ; symposia
of any other kind between men and women were unknown in
Hellas. And to what extent the influence of Greek art has
prevailed is shown by the picture of a momentary phase of
emotion in the Tomba Querciola, where a couple reclining on
the couch are kissing each other, a motive as suitable to a

---

[1] Τὴν κιθάραν στρέψας, like Apollo in the contest with Marsyas (Apollo-
dorus, *Bibliotheca* i. 4. 2).

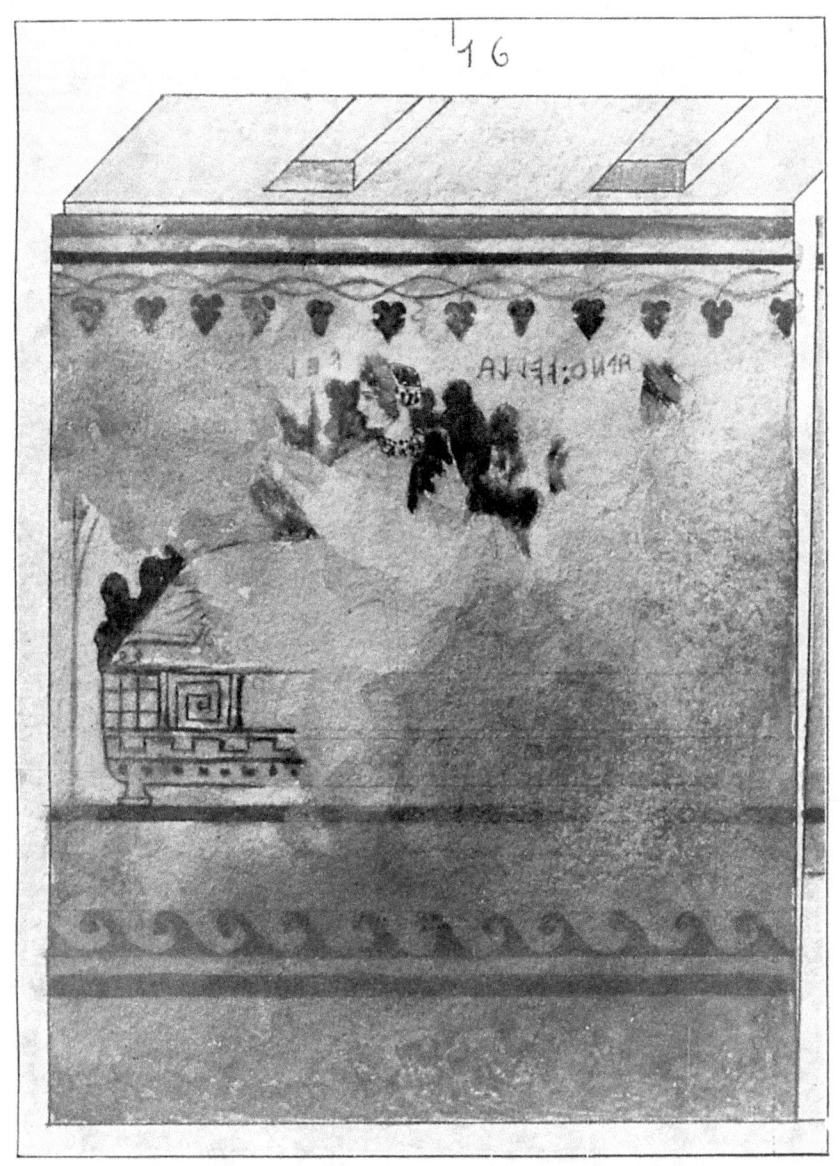

FIG. 28. ARNTH VELCHAS AND WIFE ON COUCH
PICTURE IN THE TOMBA DELL' ORCO
After a coloured drawing in the Helbig Museum

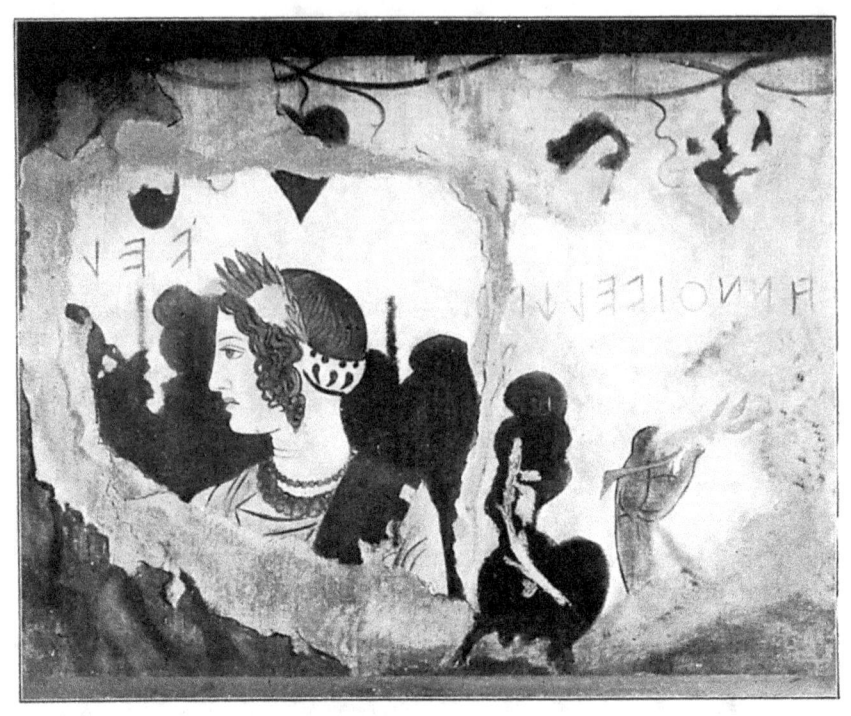

FIG. 29. HEAD OF ARNTH VELCHAS' WIFE
FROM THE TOMBA DELL' ORCO

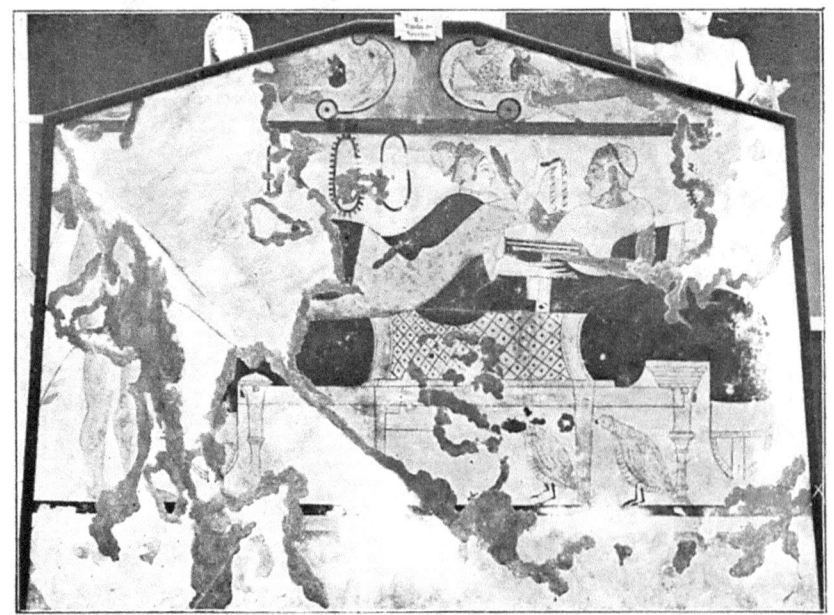

FIG. 30. BACK WALL IN THE TOMBA DEL VECCHIO

Greek hetaera picture as it is incongruous in a picture representing family life after death.[1]   Another source of error is
the pronounced sensualism of these pictures ; in a sepulchral
painting as early as the sixth century, the main picture of the
Tomba del Vecchio, we see on a banqueting-couch, under
the wreaths and chaplets with bells hanging on the wall, a
hoary old *roué* in vivacious conversation with his beautiful
young wife who holds a garland, a hypothymis, under his
nose (fig. 30).[2]   This picture is typically Etruscan in its
combination of wine and love. ' As soon as we had eaten,'
sings the Greek poet Dromon,[3] ' the slave girl removed the
tables ; one brought us water for washing, and we washed
ourselves ; then we seized again the wreaths of violets and
bound our brows with garlands.' The Etruscans seem to have
followed the Greek rules minutely, but like the Egyptians
they let the free-born women partake of the festivity of the
symposium itself.

XI

BUT we can go still further and establish beyond the
possibility of doubt that where men alone are gathered at
the symposium of eternity, the pictures represent the heads of
the families who ordered the tombs and had them decorated.
To be sure, the pictures of the sixth and the beginning of
the fifth centuries do not give us any information as to this—
even the symposium in the Tomba delle Bighe is without
inscription ; but in this respect also the sepulchral paintings
become more communicative after the middle of the fifth
century. In the Tomba Golini at Orvieto, discovered in 1863

[1] In the same picture we also find
a representation of a true Greek
motive, kottabos. Another momentary motive appears in the Tomba
d' Orfeo e d' Euridice at Corneto
(*Monumenti* v. pl. 17), a slave pulling
off his master's slippers.

[2] Hypothymides were first used ' by
the Aeolians and Ionians who wore

them round their necks, as we learn
from the poems of Anacreon and Alcaeus ' (Athenaeus xv. 678 d). Cp.
Plutarch, *Quaest. conviv.* iii. *probl.* 1, 3.
In Ionia the women perfumed their
bosoms and wore wreaths of flowers
round their ' delicate necks ', as Sappho
says (Athenaeus xv. 674 c–d).

[3] Athenaeus ix. 409 e.

and called after its discoverer, and, to judge from its style, contemporary with the Tomba degli Scudi and the front chamber of the Tomba dell' Orco, we see in the symposium on the back wall (fig. 31) two men on the same couch drinking to the accompaniment of the two familiar musicians. Beneath the couch we can make out dimly a servant, and a hunting leopard, probably feeding; both have their names attached: that of the animal is Kankru. In Egyptian reliefs also, dating from the Fifth Dynasty, we occasionally find names attached to the domestic animals depicted, for instance ducks and pigeons.

Of the two men reclining on the couch the foremost holds a drinking-bowl and an egg. In the Ny Carlsberg facsimile he is represented as beardless, but no doubt wrongly. It is an elderly man; his face is one of the earliest examples of naturalism in Etruscan portraiture. The other, full-bearded, holds a flat, fluted vessel without foot, presumably one of the celebrated Etruscan golden vessels which are more minutely characterized in a symposium in the Tomba della Pulcella; they were even introduced into Athens, where, side by side with Corinthian works in bronze, they formed part of the decoration of a wealthy house, and they are eulogized in a poem by Critias,[1] one of Athens' finest *beaux esprits*.

In this painting in the Tomba Golini the inscriptions give us much valuable information as to the connexion between the two persons.[2] Above the first we read : ' Vel lecates arnthial ruva larthialisa clan velusum nefs marniu spurana eprthnec tenve mechlum rasneas cleusinsl zilachnve pulum rumitrine thi ma[l]ce clel lur.' In translation the text runs : ' Vel Lecates, Arnth's brother,[3] son of Larth, and descendant of Vel. He held the offices of Maro urbanus (*spur* means town) and Eprthne (secular official title) and was Zilach (dictator) of the Etruscan people in Clusium . . . '

[1] Athenaeus i. 28 b.
[2] *Corpus inscr. Etrusc.* 5093-4. I am indebted to my friend, Dr. S. P. Cortsen, for help in the interpretation of this and other Etruscan inscriptions. These are for the greater part incorrectly copied in the Ny Carlsberg facsimiles.
[3] That *ruva* means brother seems to be unanimously accepted, though it only appears in the two inscriptions of this tomb.

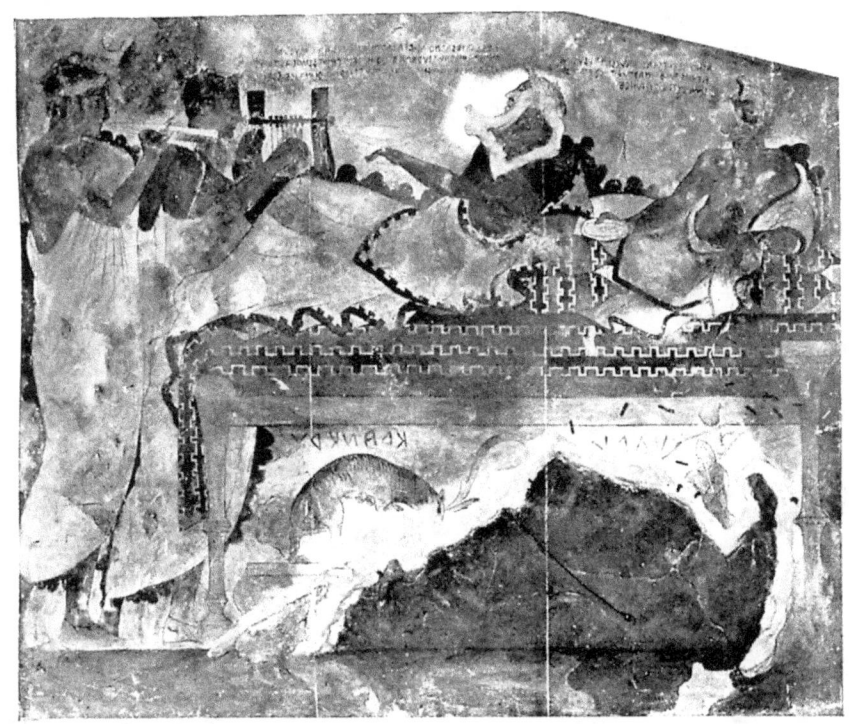

FIG. 31. SYMPOSIUM IN THE TOMBA GOLINI AT ORVIETO

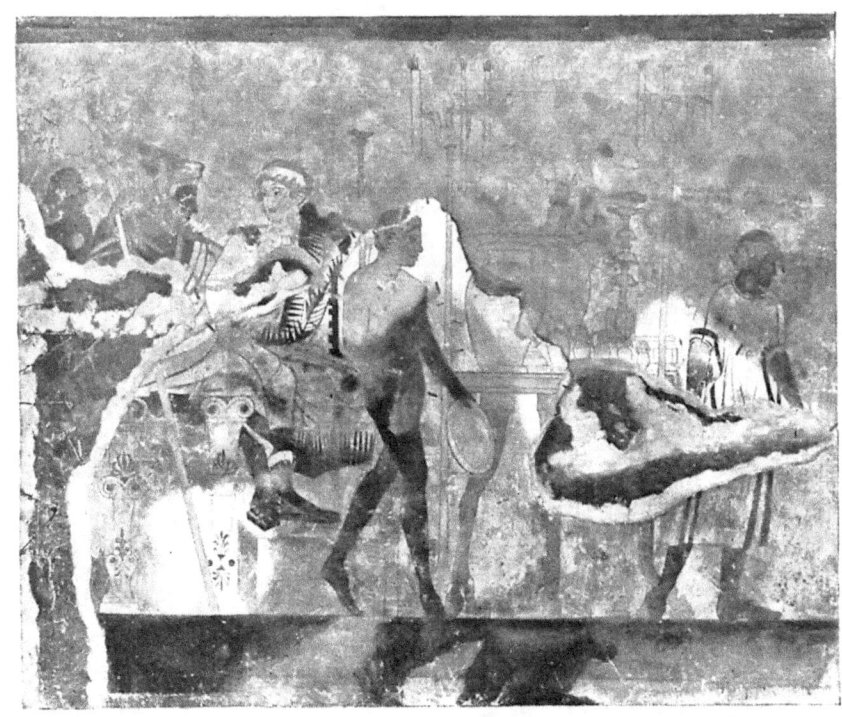

FIG. 32. WALL-PAINTING IN THE TOMBA GOLINI

The rest is unintelligible. It is interesting in the inscription to come across the name by which the Etruscans called themselves, *rasneas*; Dionysius of Halicarnassus (i. 30) was therefore justified in saying that the Etruscans called themselves Rasenas. The name Larth is common in Etruscan inscriptions. The Romans knew it and called the well-known Etruscan king by his full name, Lars Porsenna (in Etruscan, Larth Pursna).[1]

We now turn to the inscription above the bearded man on the same couch; his name is Arnth Leinies, son of Larth, and descendant of Vel; his official titles follow, and the inscription ends: 'ru[va] l[ecates velus] amce,' i. e., was brother of Vel Lecates. Thus we have two brothers reclining on the same couch, and the inscription makes it probable that the other symposiasts, too, are not chance revellers, but members of the same family, united in the picture as they were in life and in the grave.

In the same tomb, to the left of this scene, we see a table, bearing several metal vessels, a thymiaterion, and an ivory box for incense, and flanked by two candelabra with lighted candles stuck into birds' beaks (fig. 32). The Etruscans were considered inventors of the art of candle-making and taught the Romans to manufacture different kinds of candles, from big wax candles—candelae and cerei—to cheap dips—sebaceae. The Italic peoples used candles and candlesticks until Roman Imperial times, though in the last centuries they also had oil lamps, the manufacture and use of which they had learned from the Greeks; the oldest clay lamps found in the northern part of Italy date from about 300 B.C.[2] To the left of the table is seen a naked slave with a jug and a dish; to the right a young man in a light-coloured, sleeved chiton, who has been conjectured

---

[1] The name Pursna or Pursena has, however, never been found in any Etruscan inscription. The Etruscan Lar or Larth has nothing to do with the Roman Las or Lar. Cp. Schulze, *Zur Geschichte latein. Eigennamen*, 85.

1; Pauli, *Altital. Studien*, iv. 64 ff.
[2] With reference to the use of tapers at the bier in antiquity see Rushforth, *Journal of Roman Studies*, v. 1915, p. 149 ff.

to be another servant. But again the inscription affords positive information : 'Vel leinies larthial ruva arnthialum clan velusum prumaths avils semphs lupuce'; i.e. 'Vel Leinies, Larth's brother, son of Arnth and descendant of Vel; he died (*lupuce*) at the age of 7.'[1] So the boy is son of the hindmost man on the banqueting-couch and belongs to the noble family interred in the tomb.

XII

CORRESPONDING to the lassoing of the horse in the Tomba del Morente, as a preparation for the chariot race, we find in the Tomba Golini pictures of the preparations for the banquet which is celebrated in the pictures mentioned above. In one of the pictures we see cattle, venison, and poultry hanging in the larder, in another the cooking in the kitchen itself (fig. 33); like everything else in Etruria, it is accompanied by the flute. To the left of the flute-player a woman is struggling with a sideboard piled with food; to the right a naked slave with a loincloth is working at a small table, using two small implements rather like plummets. Various interpretations have been advanced : that he is kneading dough, or grinding colours; the latter explanation, however, is improbable in a kitchen scene. Besides these Dennis proposes a third possibility—that he is chopping vegetables, but he dares not commit himself to a decision. The table itself, at which the slave is standing, seems to have a raised edge, and thereby recalls the elder Cato's recipe for the preparation of cheese cakes and puffs[2] : 'Take a clean table, a foot broad, surround it with an edge (*balteus*), and then mix honey and cheese on it.' For puffs, directions are given to belabour the dough with two sticks or staves (*rudes*). After all the procedure here is somewhat

[1] Cp. Vilh. Thomsen, *Remarques sur la parenté de la langue étrusque, Bulletin de l'Académie royale de Danemark,* 1899, no. 4, p. 391.
[2] *De agricultura* 76 and 86.

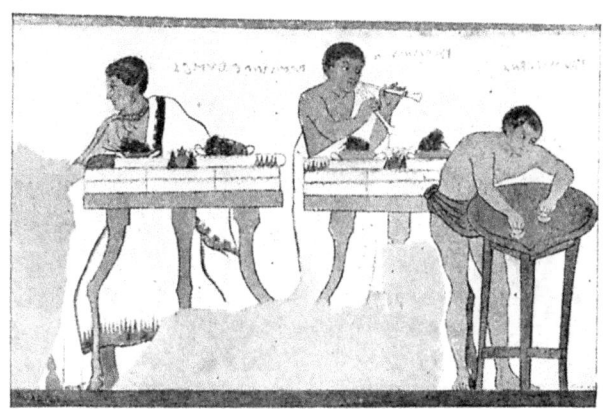

FIG. 33

KITCHEN INTERIOR IN THE TOMBA GOLINI

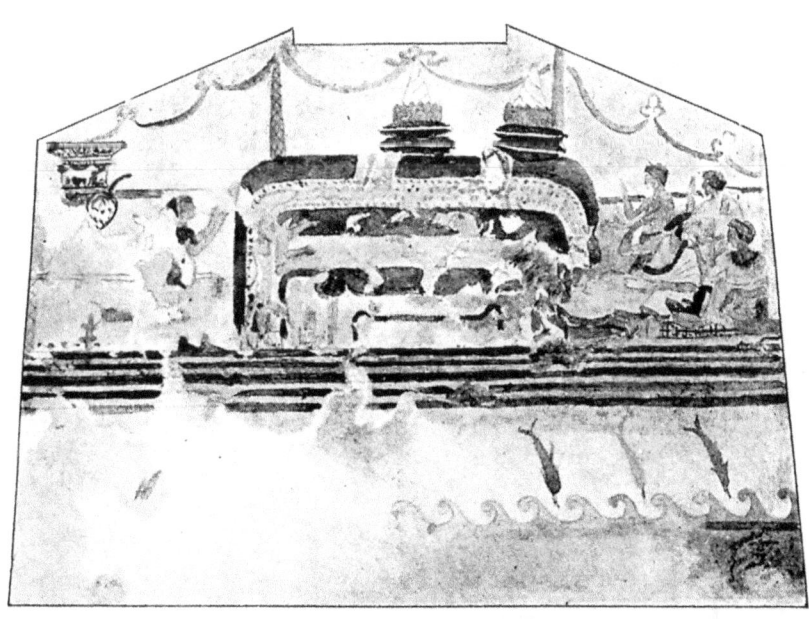

FIG. 34. PAINTING IN THE TOMBA DEL LETTO FUNEBRE

After a coloured drawing in the Helbig Museum

similar, only that the dough is kneaded with pieces of metal and not with staves.

In these scenes from kitchen and wine-cellar, where the wood is being chopped,[1] where the cooks are swinging the saucepans or working at the range,[2] where young slaves are struggling with sideboards covered with drinking-vessels, the inscriptions contain the names of the slaves. Men desired to be served in the after-life by the same skilful slaves as in the present, and it was therefore the custom in later times to add the names. This reminds one of the Egyptian tomb-reliefs, where sometimes the serfs and the slave girls are designated only by the name and mark of the estate, so that in a way each of them represents one of the estates of the deceased lord, whereas in other cases they have their proper names attached and survive as personalities in the after-life.

XIII

THUS we see a slow transformation taking place in the ideas which inspired the Etruscan tomb-paintings. In the Tomba del Morto and the Tomba degli Auguri, the representation of the death lament showed plainly that the main theme was the festival in honour of the dead ; and the memorial feast itself should probably in most cases be recognized in the banquet accompanied by the symposium or—as in the Tomba delle Iscrizioni—the preparations for it. This conception is also clearly expressed in the sepulchral paintings of the fifth century B.C., such as the Tomba del Letto funebre, where the main picture (fig. 34) represents an enormous couch with a footstool in front[3] ; on the tall

---

[1] Cp. Plautus, *Pseudolus* 158 'te cum securi caudicali praeficio provinciae.'

[2] Cp. Seneca, *Epist.* 114. 26 'adspice culinas nostras et concursantis inter tot ignes coquos.'

[3] Footstools were also used in Rome for mounting the high couches. Varro, *De lingua Latina* v. 168.

pile of bolsters and coverlets rest two pairs of cushions, each of them supporting a green chaplet encircling a pointed cap (*tutulus*). Green festoons and a long red cord hang on the walls : to the right of the couch are two symposiasts and two slaves ; the slaves face the big central couch, and hold one an egg, the other a loaf in their raised hands. To the left of the picture are the flute-player and the sideboard with vases. Here we get an idea how a lectisternium was spread in honour of the dead, in connexion with the symposium at a memorial feast. The dead are represented by their head-gear ; to that the slaves to the right are offering sacrifice, to that the flute-player to the left sounds his notes. How deeply, in this direction also, tradition influenced the Romans, and how long the practice lingered, is seen from the description which the satirist Persius gives (iii. 103) of a noble Roman lying in state :

Hinc tuba, candelae, tandemque beatulus alto
compositus lecto crassisque lutatus amomis
in portam rigidas calces extendit : at illum
hesterni capite induto subiere Quirites.

And then the horns, the candles ! and the dead,
Smeared with thick balms, lies stiff on lofty bed,
Heels pointing doorwards, till he's borne away
By new-capped citizens [1] of yesterday.

But the pictures in the Tomba Golini seem to indicate that the symposium is not only a ceremony on the funeral day or at memorial feasts, but that the purpose is, by means of the painting as well as by the undoubtedly splendid accessories of the tombs, which were rifled and removed long ago, to secure to the dead or the whole of the family, who in course of time were interred in the tomb, a happy and festive existence hereafter ; the same idea as in the Egyptian tomb-reliefs, the object of which was to safeguard the deceased against 'the second death', that is, annihilation. And just as the Egyptian tomb-reliefs extend to all aspects

[1] i.e. slaves made free by his will, and entitled to wear the cap of liberty.

of life in order that the dead may enjoy without restriction the sight of everything which made his life rich and festive, from the industry of the slaves and artisans occupied in his service to his own boating and hunting expeditions in the papyrus thickets of the Nile, so the Etruscan sepulchral paintings have a further object and treat subjects which are only intelligible if the end in view is to procure for the dead a full enjoyment of the delights of life, and which cannot in any way be associated with funeral or funeral feast. This applies especially to the hunting pictures of the sixth and fifth centuries B.C., found respectively in the Tomba della Caccia e della Pesca and in the Tomba Querciola.

XIV

IN the older group of tombs of the latter part of the sixth and the earlier part of the fifth centuries B.C. we find a bright and cheerful delight in the material pleasures of life, and a clear confidence in the belief that the race, whose means are sufficient to provide and adorn a sumptuous sepulchral chamber, will also be permitted to enjoy all this—from wine and women to hunting and sanguinary games—in the hereafter. Thus it is not for nothing that these tombs synchronize with the time of Etruscan imperialism. Previous to this, the maritime power of Etruria had made it dreaded and hated by the Greeks, whose ships were exposed to seizure and piracy as often as they ventured across the ' Tyrrhenian Sea ', so that the Greeks had only one colony on the north coast of Sicily, and had great trouble in keeping up communications with the Campanian Kyme and with Massilia.[1] ' The savage Etruscan ' already appears in post-Homeric poetry, where Circe bears Odysseus two children, Latinus and Agrius (the savage), who represent the two

[1] Strabo vi. p. 410 (=Ephorus, *fragm.* 2 in Müller, *Fragmenta historic. graec.* i. p. 246). The ingenious ety- mologist Philochorus even derived the word ' tyrant ' from Tyrrhenians (Philoch. *fragm.* 5 in Müller, *op. cit.*).

principal races of Italy, the Latins and the Etruscans. At
length, in 474 B.C., the Kymeans, in alliance with Hieron,
the ruler of Syracuse, succeeded in gaining a sea victory
over the Etruscan fleet, which Pindar has celebrated in the
first Pythian Ode (i. 72 ff.), and after which Hieron sent to
Olympia a bronze helmet with an inscription recording the
victory, now in the British Museum. This defeat was the
first warning that the Etruscans had reached the zenith of
their power, but as late as the latter part of the fourth century
their piracy was still dangerous and troublesome to Greek
shipping, as is seen from a passage of Aristotle and an inscription of 325–324 B.C.[1] As a bulwark of their maritime power,
as early as the sixth century they had conquered Corsica,
and on land they ruled from the plain of the Po, which they
likewise conquered in the sixth century, to the southernmost
part of Campania, where they made Capua itself submit to
their power.[2] Cato was justified in saying that almost the
whole of Italy in the days of old had been ‘ in the power of
the Tuscans ’,[3] and when Sophocles [4] would enumerate the
districts of Italy he mentions only three : Oinotria (South
Italy), the Tyrrhenian, and the Ligurian land. When the
Athenians during the Peloponnesian War undertook the
desperate campaign against Syracuse, they allied themselves
in 415 with the Etruscans, whose auxiliaries were amongst
the bravest in the Athenian offensive force.[5] In the period
of the wall-paintings in question, Rome herself was also
made subject to them and had to pay contributions to the
powerful Etruscan confederation, after the king of Clusium,
Porsenna, had seized the city in 508 B.C. As is well known,
attempts were made by later historians to gloss over this
capture of the town, and the honorary decrees of the senate
to Porsenna are described as voluntary, but tell quite plainly
their own tale of subjection.[6] Against the background of

[1] Dittenberger, *Sylloge inscriptionum Graecarum*,[3] 305, with note 1.
[2] Polybius ii. 17. Livy v. 33. 7–8.
[3] *Origines* 62.
[4] Dionys. Halic. i. 12.
[5] Thucydides vi. 88, and vii. 54–5.
[6] Dionys. Halic. v. 26, 35, 39.

this event the contemporary Tomba della Scimmia at Chiusi acquires a new interest ; it was constructed for one of those families which took part in the victory over Rome. But previous to this, the names of the Roman kings : Lucius Tarquinius and Tarquinius Superbus—Tarquinius is the Etruscan Tarchna [1]—bear witness to the dependence of Rome, which is also evident from the permanent Etruscan occupation of the Janiculum. It is quite possible that the expulsion of Tarquinius Superbus does not mark the fall of the national monarchy, but was simply an attempt to throw off the foreign yoke, an attempt which led to Porsenna's occupation of the city two years later and thus did not bring about the emancipation of the Romans.[2] It is in this period of dependence that the Etruscans left their mark on the laws and customs of Rome, that the three oldest Roman tribes, Ramnes, Tities, and Luceres, got their names, which, as stated by Varro,[3] on the evidence of an Etruscan tragedian Volnius, are Etruscan, a view shared by the modern philologist Wilhelm Schulze.[4] The insignia also of the Roman officials, such as the curule chair and the toga praetexta,[5] and the twelve consular lictors with the fasces,[6] are rightly traced back to Etruria. For the Etruscan confederation consisted of twelve towns, and each of these chose a king who appeared at the gatherings followed by a lictor, and only when they chose a common overlord and war-leader could he appear with twelve lictors. It is therefore rather improbable that the Roman kings appeared with twelve lictors in their train ; more probably this large retinue only became the privilege of the *consuls* after the suppression of Etruria. But it was upon the nobility of Rome that those years of Etruscan predominance left their deepest impress, and it has thus been possible for Wilhelm Schulze, through his investigations of Etruscan and Latin proper names, to

[1] Schulze, *Zur Geschichte latein. Eigennamen*, p. 95 f., 262 ff.
[2] Dionys. Halic. iii. 45, 47 ff.
[3] Varro, *De lingua Latina* v. 5;
Livy i. 13. 8.
[4] Cp. E. Kornemann, *Klio* xiv. 1914–15, p. 190. [5] Livy i. 8. 3.
[6] Dionys. Halic. iii. 61–2.

throw a remarkable light on the earliest history of Rome and to prove that a great number of the oldest patrician families of Rome were descendants of the Etruscan ruling race, and that intermarriage with Etruscans, and Etruscan influence on Rome, persisted down to the end of the Roman republic.[1] It is also beyond doubt that the peculiar Roman system of patron and client, by which clients attached themselves to a nobleman as followers (*cluentes*), added his name to their own, and paid him dues in peace time, though they were originally immune from military service,[2] was of Etruscan origin, nay, was the essential feature in the structure of the Etruscan community. In course of time the Roman clients became liable to military service, obtaining at the same time civic rights, and it is presumably this fact which accounts for Rome's final victory over the Etruscans, whose proud Lucumones reserved to themselves both civic privileges and military skill, and were therefore doomed to extinction when luxury and effeminacy had sapped their strength.

But at the period of the tombs in question the blood of the nobility is still healthy and is in no need of regeneration. This is the nobility whose long lances controlled Italy, and whose cavalry was so terrible in onset.[3] The pictures of the tombs show them at the death lament, at feasts, and on hunting expeditions, at symposia, where men and women freely indulge in wine and love, and finally in the Tomba delle Bighe as spectators seated on the stands. On the other hand, the horsemen, the dancers, the dancing-women, and the athletes are certainly of lower extraction, hired servants like the corresponding performers in Rome, perhaps, to some extent, clients.

[1] Wilhelm Schulze, *Zur Geschichte lateinischer Eigennamen. Abh. der kgl. Gesellsch. der Wissensch. zu Göttingen, Phil.-hist. Kl.*, Neue Folge, Bd. 5, No. 5, p. 62 ff.

[2] Dionys. Halic. ii. 8, 10.
[3] Livy iv. 18. 8. Cp. ix. 29. 2, where the Etruscans are described as the most dangerous enemies of the Romans.

XV

But domestic and foreign enemies destroyed this race of rulers. At the beginning of the fourth century they were attacked simultaneously by the Gauls from the north, by the Samnites [1] from the south-east, and by the Romans from the south. The Gauls inundated for some time the whole of Etruria and presently captured Rome as well, but were driven back again to North Italy. The Samnites seized Capua ; but a far heavier blow was the loss of the great city of Veii, the southernmost city of Etruria proper, which was captured by the Romans in 396 B.C. [2] In spite of the alliance with Carthage, the maritime power of the Etruscans also declined in the course of the fourth century, but it was not until the third century that they received the death-blow at the hands of the Romans and Latins. That they were still dangerous antagonists at the beginning of the third century may be seen from Livy's account, but at the end of the century, during the second Punic war, their rebellious spirit was easily quelled, and even Hannibal could not tempt them to unite in revolt. [3] At that time the country was still rich, as is plainly shown by the requisitions for Scipio's army. [4] It was not until the following century that Etruria sank into deep poverty ; in the time of the Gracchi the country was almost a waste. [5] Plautus describes the Etruscan people as very immoral; in the *Cistellaria* (562) the poet speaks of those who procure their dowry ignobly, like the Tuscans, by selling their bodies, and in the *Curculio* (482) the Etruscan quarter of Rome is referred to as ' inhabited by persons who sell themselves '. Then followed in the first century B.C. the military colonies of Sulla, [6] which gradually Romanized the country. Inscriptions, especially from the borderland of Umbria, which had been partly Etruscan, bear

[1] Livy iv. 37. 1–2.
[2] Livy v. 22. 8.
[3] Livy xxvii. 21. 6 ; 38. 6.
[4] Livy xxviii. 45. 14–18.

[5] Plutarch, *Tiberius Gracchus* 8.
[6] As a punishment because the country had joined the party of Marius. Plutarch, *Marius* 41.

ample witness to the way in which the language changed even within the old Etruscan families. About the middle of the first century parts of the country were ravaged by P. Clodius Pulcher and his bands of soldiers.[1] Then comes the foundation of new military colonies by Caesar and, finally, the complete Romanization of the country under Augustus. Propertius [2] describes, not without pathos, the extermination of the last Etruscan strongholds during the Perusian war in the year 40 B.C.: 'eversosque focos antiquae gentis Etruscae'.

The knowledge of the Etruscan language was preserved all through antiquity by the Etruscan soothsayers. The emperor Claudius was versed in Etruscan, and delivered a long address in the Senate about the preservation of the old Etruscan ritual against the invasion of new, oriental elements. The other emperors had, as a rule, an Etruscan soothsayer in their suite, whom they consulted before taking any important step, and this custom survived down to the introduction of Christianity. Julian the Apostate was accompanied by hosts of Etruscan soothsayers, who, however, undoubtedly read the sacred books in the Latin translation by Tarquitius Priscus,[3] and, as late as 408, we learn that Tuscan soothsayers and scribes still existed. If any of them at that time could still read the language, then Etruscan, as a dead and sacred language, had survived the disappearance of the people by about half a millennium.[4]

---

[1] Cicero, *Pro Milone* 26, 74, 87.

[2] ii. 1.29. The later authors speak of nothing but the corpulency and imbecility of the Etruscans. Catullus, *Carm.* 39. 21. Virgil, *Georg.* ii. 193; *Aen.* xi. 732. Diodorus v. 40.

[3] Thulin, Pauly-Wissowa, vii. 2434.

[4] The best summary view of the Etruscan civilization is still to be found in Ottfried Müller, *Die Etrusker*, in the second edition by Deecke.

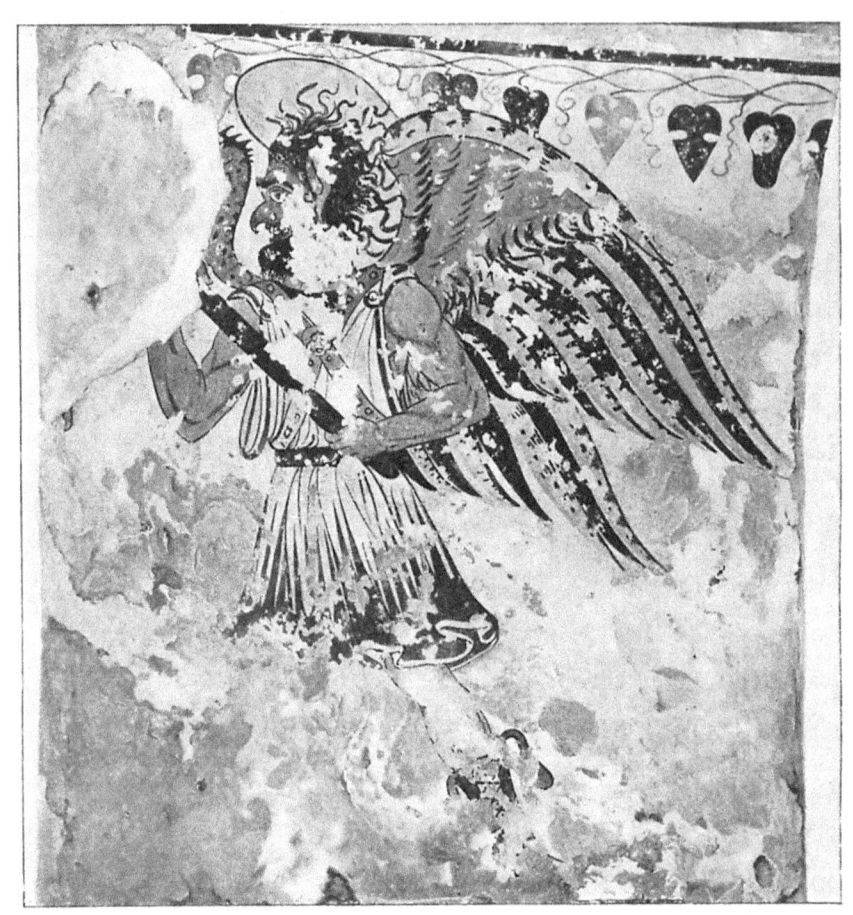

Fig. 35. DEMON IN THE TOMBA DELL' ORCO

XVI

To this long, sad period of national decline the later group of Etruscan tomb-paintings and reliefs on cinerary urns form a remarkable and melancholy accompaniment.

The continuity is unbroken; the new creeps in, at first, without superseding the old subjects. This is especially clear in the front room of the Tomba dell' Orco, which dates from the latter part of the fifth century, and from which we reproduced the beautiful married couple at the symposium (figs. 28, 29); in the same sepulchral chamber we see in a corner, beneath a finely stylized vine, a terrible death demon, with large wings and a shock of wildly fluttering reddish hair, which is sharply outlined on a blue background as if it were surrounded by a halo. His beard is pointed, his nose terminates in an eagle's beak; over his shoulder a snake rears itself, and the latchets of his shoes are snakes. His dress consists of a sleeved chiton with belt and shoulder-straps, and in his hand he carries a torch or a hammer. The eyes roll horribly in the bluish face; the colour of the skin recalls the blue-bottle fly (fig. 35).

This death demon is painted isolated, unconnected with the subjects of the rest of the paintings, and could indeed be explained away as a decorative figure, created, to be sure, by an imagination inflamed with terror. But in the third room of the same tomb, the pictures of which belong to the transition from the fifth to the fourth century, a similar demon of the nether world is already represented in action (fig. 36). The inscription gives his name, Tuchulcha; he has asses' ears, two snakes rear themselves like horns above his brow, and with a huge snake he threatens a long-haired youth who sits sorrowful on the rock, with a himation round his loins; his name, according to the inscription, is ' These '. He is the Greek Theseus, and the young man opposite to him is Pirithous; the motive is their sufferings in the

Underworld, where they had ventured down in order to abduct Persephone. But there broods over the scene a sinister spirit which is not Greek. Thus we see behind the rock on which Theseus is seated a loathsome snake with winged head, and the remains of a blue demon with staff and chiton, a kinsman of Tuchulcha. The appearance, to the left of this weird phantasmagoria, of the peaceful sideboard with its fine metal bowls [1] and with a handsome naked slave as cup-bearer in front of it, has undeniably a somewhat odd effect. This is a reminiscence of the old joyous symposium scenes, and a remarkable witness to the lack of clearness in the Etruscan mind and to the fragmentary character of Etruscan pictorial art. A similar mixture of everyday life and myth would be inconceivable in Egyptian or in Greek art.

Similarly, in the Tomba Golini, we see the side-table and the slave in immediate continuation of the picture representing the two enthroned rulers of the Underworld—Hades and Persephone (inscriptions: Eita and Phersipnai). Hades has a wolf-helmet and a snake-sceptre and is caressing Persephone, who has a bird-crowned sceptre in her left hand, and rests her right hand on the knee of Hades (see above fig. 32). Her dress, her face, and her yellow hair under the golden diadem are all splendidly painted.

In later Etruscan paintings we come upon two new groups of motives—fantastic pictures of the Underworld, and scenes from Greek mythology. Sometimes they mingle as in the Theseus and Pirithous scene and in the pictures of Hades and Persephone. Hades and Persephone recur in a painting in the third chamber of the Tomba dell' Orco (inscription: Aita and Phersipnei), where weird mists roll about them, and a figure with three heads, Gerun, is standing before their throne (fig. 37). It is the Geryon of the Greeks, but he is not the cowherd on the far-distant island Erythra, but a warrior in complete armour who seems to be receiving the commands of Hades. Evidently the Etruscans

[1] Cp. for the well-appointed table Plautus's description of a liberal host (*Menaechmi* 102): 'tantas struices concinnat patinarias.'

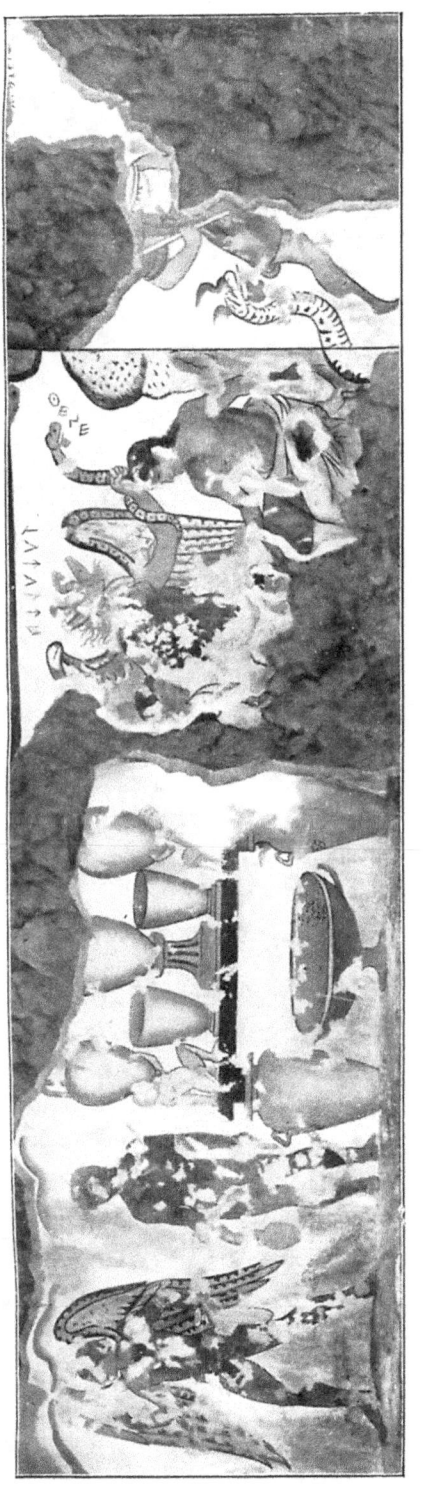

FIG. 36. PICTURE IN THE TOMBA DELL' ORCO AT CORNETO

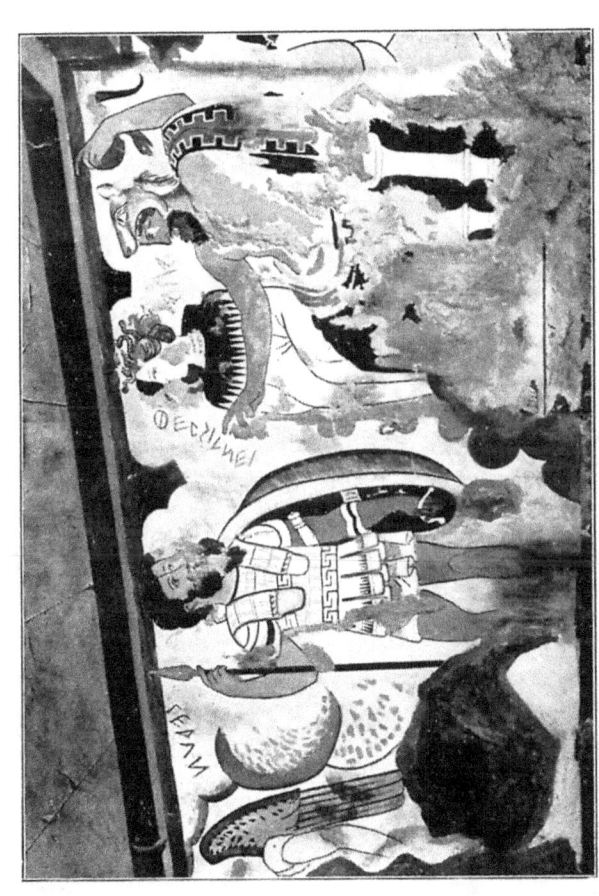

FIG. 37. HADES, PERSEPHONE AND GERYON IN
THE TOMBA DELL' ORCO

have made him the servant and champion of Hades. Persephone has snakes in her hair and a curious collar which we meet again on the chitons of women in white Attic lekythoi of the fifth century B.C.[1] Hades wears the traditional wolf-helmet. It is remarkable that a head exactly similar to that of Hades is found among Michelangelo's sketches (fig. 38), which seems to indicate that Michelangelo somewhere in Tuscany saw and sketched an old Etruscan tomb. To be sure, the snout of the animal reminds one of a pig's, but the long ears and the fur are those of the wolf.

In the other paintings of the Tomba dell' Orco we meet furthermore with Agamemnon in the underworld, and in front of him Tiresias (Hinthial Teriasals it reads, i.e. the shade of Tiresias). But in the second chamber of this tomb, dating from the fourth century B.C., there is also a scene from Greek mythology which has nothing to do with death and the underworld ; Odysseus blinding the Cyclops Polyphemus (inscriptions : Uthuste and Cuclu). We can here speak of a renaissance, in so far as a scene from a Greek myth formed the subject of the big picture

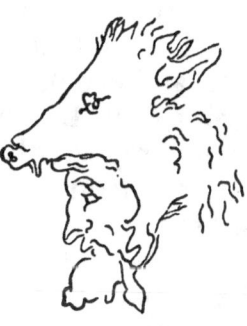

Fig. 38.

of the beginning of the sixth century in the Tomba dei Tori (cp. fig. 2). But the aim of the later school of Etruscan painters is not so much to adorn the tomb with a beautiful decorative panel after some Greek prototype ; on the contrary, they turn to the Greek myths for the sake of their subjects and pick out motives which also give expression to the curious strain of cruelty inherent in the Etruscan mind.

This is seen most clearly in the famous picture from the François tomb at Vulci, discovered in 1857 by the Italian painter Alessandro François. The Ny Carlsberg Glyptotek possesses a facsimile, executed by the painter Mariani after the original in the Palazzo Torlonia, whither the Prince Torlonia had it removed together with other wall-paintings

[1] Walther Riezler, *Weissgründige attische Lekythen*, pl. 70.

from the same tomb : but the copy is too smooth to be trustworthy. Unfortunately, permission to obtain another copy from the inaccessible Palazzo is certainly not to be had. The picture (fig. 39) represents the sacrifice of Trojan captives on the grave of Patroclus. Achilles (Etruscan Achle) slaughters with his own hands the captured Trojans (Etruscan Truials) ; Ajax, son of Oileus (Aivas Vilatas), and Ajax, son of Telamon (Aivas Tlamunus) stand by ; Agamemnon (Achmemrun) is also present, and the shade of Patroclus, thirsting for the blood (Hinthial Patrucles), as well as two truly Etruscan figures, a female winged genius of death, Vanth, and the Etruscan death-god, Charun, coloured like the blue-bottle fly, with hammer uplifted.

This subject was chosen for the sake of the slaughter.[1] Sex and cruelty are, to use a chemical expression, the ' basic group ' of the Etruscan mind. Thus the same subject is found repeatedly on Etruscan sarcophagi and vases, and in the relief on a cinerary urn, and may be compared with the most common and popular representation in Etruscan reliefs : Eteocles and Polynices killing each other. Even a motive like Ajax falling on his own sword constantly recurs in Etruscan art, as well as the barbarous subject, maschalismos (maiming of slain enemies), which is especially common on Etruscan gems.[2] A characteristic feature of the picture in the François tomb is the deep wounds in the legs of the Trojan captives ; they are meant to prevent attempts to escape and were evidently in keeping with Etruscan custom. For stress is laid on the cruelty of the Etruscans towards prisoners of war by Greek as well as by Latin authors ; thus, as early as the fifth century, the inhabitants of Caere, after a sea victory, stoned to death their Phocaean captives[3] ; and yet Strabo writes of the Caeretans that they were highly respected for their bravery and love of justice, and because,

[1] It is to be observed that the Etruscans thrust with the sword ; this also the Romans inherited ; whereas the Gauls cut and the Iberians thrust as well as cut. Polybius ii. 33. 6, and iii. 114.

[2] Cp. Beazley, *Lewes House Collection of Gems*, p. 38, 74 f.

[3] Herodotus i. 167.

powerful as they were, they refrained from piracy. The Romans knew better when they personified Etruscan cruelty in Mezentius, King of Caere, who had living and dead tied together to rot side by side ; nor did the Romans ever forget that the inhabitants of Tarquinii once slaughtered three hundred and seven Roman captives,[1] and they took bloody revenge on them. The Greeks also knew of the massacring of prisoners of war, but they always cherished scruples about it and felt qualms, as when Themistocles was compelled to pay a tribute of slain captives to ' Dionysius, the eater of raw flesh '.[2]

Before we leave the François tomb we must remind the reader of the existence of a remarkable series of pictures with subjects taken from the conflicts between Etruria and Rome in the time of the Roman kings.[3]

XVII

THE demons of the Underworld who figure in the Etruscan paintings are almost all sinister. The devils brandishing torches and snakes, familiar both from the paintings and from the reliefs on the cinerary urns, remind one of Livy's [4] description of the fight of the Tarquinians and the Faliscans against the Romans in 354 B.C., when a troop of Etruscan priests, armed with flaming torches and live snakes, threw themselves in ecstatic fury on the Roman armies, who received them undauntedly and won the day. Charun, also, is a common figure on the Etruscan sarcophagi and cinerary urns of the fourth and following centuries, suggesting by his colour the demon of putrefaction, Eurynomus, whom Polygnotus had painted, in his great picture of the Underworld in the Lesche of the Cnidians at Delphi, seated snarling on the skin of a carrion-vulture, his flesh the

---

[1] Livy vii. 15. 10 ; 19. 3.   xii. 1897, p. 58 ff.
[2] Plutarch, *Themistocles* 13.   [4] Livy vii. 17. 3–5. Cp. iv. 33. 2.
[3] Körte, *Jahrbuch des archäol. Instit.*

colour of a blue-bottle fly.[1] Charun, therefore, is not identical
with the old ferryman, Charon, of the Greeks ; he is the
messenger of death, the terrible fetcher of souls, like Charos
in the popular Greek belief of our own day. Only the
'Charon door' of the Greek theatre indicates the existence
of similar popular ideas among the ancient Greeks.

The winged Vanth in the François tomb seems to be
one of the benevolent demons of the underworld, the Lasas.
Such a one also appears in a door panel in the Tomba Golini,
already frequently cited : here she has wings, snakes in
her girdle, and a scroll in her hand (fig. 40). She is
evidently either receiving or escorting the dead, a young man
in a mantle, who stands in a biga with running horses ; in
the inscription above him the word Larth can easily be read,
proving that he is not a professional charioteer, but a young
man of high standing. His arrival in the underworld is
greeted by a trumpeter, painted over the door. We may
notice here that the 'Tyrrhenian trumpet' was famous far
and wide and was even introduced into Greece ; it is mentioned several times in Greek tragedies.[2] The curved
trumpet here seen is also depicted on a wall in the Tomba
degli Scudi at Corneto and, like the curved staff of the augurs,
was adopted by the Romans, who designated both of them
by the name of lituus ; Cicero maintains that the lituus-
trumpet was the earlier of the two and gave its form and name
to the lituus-staff, the badge of the augurs. The introduction
of the lituus-staff was attributed to Romulus, and his sacred
staff was said to have been rediscovered by a miracle in the
time of Camillus.[3]

The scroll in the hand of the female demon, referred to
above, presumably contained an account of the good actions
of the dead, to be used when he presented himself before the
throne of Hades. The good genius herself is seen at work
in a small panel of the Tomba degli Scudi, where she is

[1] Pausanias x. 28. 7–8.   [3] Cicero, *De divinatione* i. 30. Plu-
[2] Sophocles, *Ajax* 17. Aeschylus,   tarch, *Camillus* 32.
Eumenides 567. Euripides, *Rhesus* 988.

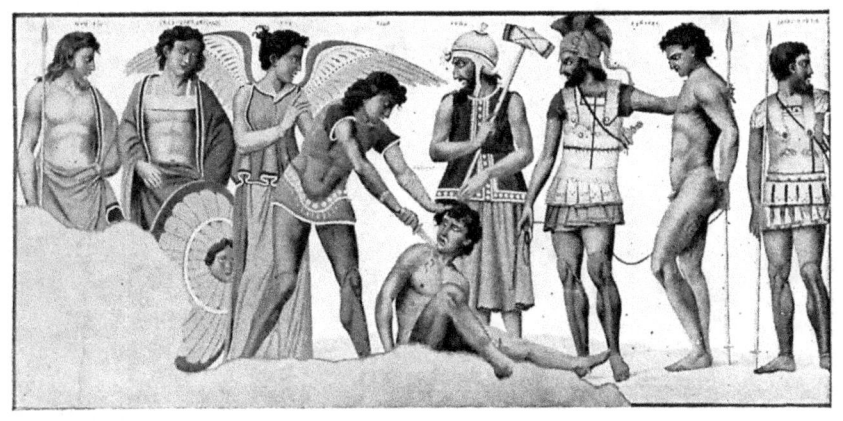

FIG. 39. WALL-PAINTING FROM THE TOMBA FRANÇOIS AT VULCI

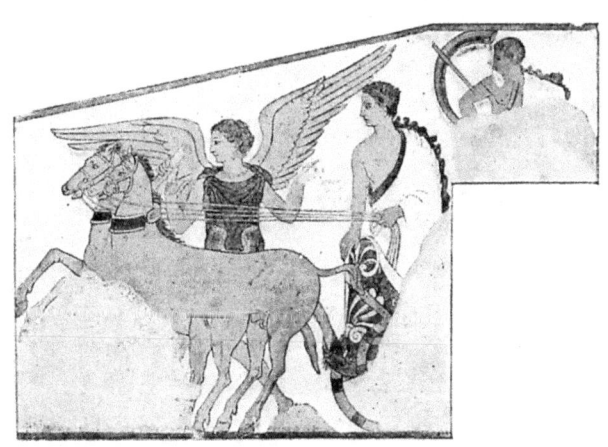

FIG. 40. PAINTING IN THE TOMBA GOLINI AT ORVIETO

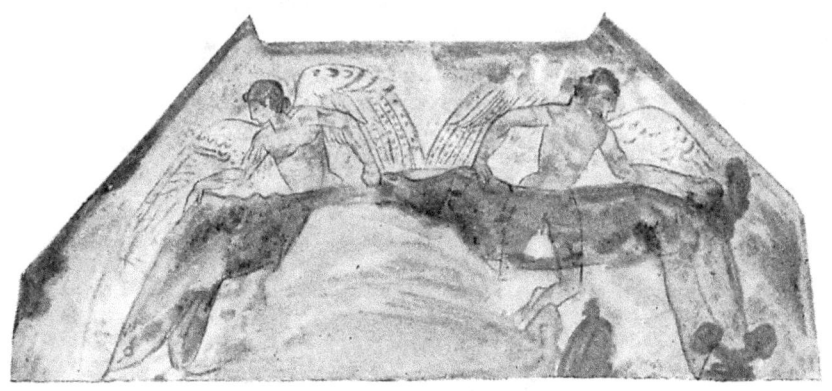

FIG. 41. PAINTING FROM THE TOMBA DELLA PULCELLA

scratching an inscription on a tablet (cp. fig. 27), while another holds a torch upside down. Both these figures are repeated in the reliefs of the Etruscan cinerary urns and pass directly into the plastic art of Roman sarcophagi as two allegorical figures: Fama, who writes the merits of the dead on a tablet, and the genius of Death with torch inverted.

A couple of flying genii appear already in the Tomba della Pulcella, which belongs to the first half of the fifth century, in the pointed pediment above the recess in which the ashes of the dead were deposited. They carry between them a cloth which they seem to be laying down, probably the cerecloth for the dead (fig. 41).[1] Perhaps this also explains the mysterious scene, figured on two tomb altars from Chiusi, one of which is in the Barracco Collection (fig. 42), the other in the Ny Carlsberg Glyptotek (Catalogue No. H. 76). The motives of the reliefs on these limestone altars from Chiusi and on the cinerary urns from the same town, all dating from the sixth century, are taken from the funeral, like the subjects in the contemporary tomb-paintings, and represent the lament of men and women over the dead on the bier, the burial feast and the preparations for it, and the wild dancing-scenes at the funeral. It may thus be that the scene on the relief illustrated, which seems to give a picture of the women's quarters, represents the women of the house in the act of scrutinizing and choosing the cerecloth for the deceased; meanwhile, the house was probably draped with cloth, and the dwellers of the house put on mourning. Presumably the mourning colour of the Etruscans was white, like that of the Romans at a later date; when in mourning, the women of Rome, to the wonder of Plutarch, assumed white dresses and white headgear, at the same time loosening their hair.[2] The hair flowing down upon the shoulders is also frequently seen in reliefs on cinerary urns. But there is still something mysterious in this motive, and an examination of the mutilated

---

[1] An Etruscan gem shows the dead Ajax and a winged genius in the act of placing the cerecloth over him.

Beazley, *The Lewes House Collection of Ancient Gems*, p. 34, no. 37.

[2] Plutarch, *Aetia romana* 26 and 14.

ash urn in the Museum of Chiusi (fig. 43) does not make it
any clearer. This urn has hitherto been explained as representing a marriage scene. But as the opposite side of the
urn represents scenes at the door of the tomb, it is more
natural to interpret this relief also as a death scene ; the
flute-player and the two men with laurel branches we know
from the funeral ceremonies (cp. p. 19), and the curious scene
to the right, where two men draw a fringed cloth like a
baldachin over a veiled centre figure, each of whose arms is
held by two side figures (probably a man and a woman),
might then be conjectured to represent a sort of symbolic
interment where the dead is placed in a sitting posture,
supported by the family, instead of the normal posture,
full length on the bier.

It is to be hoped that future investigation may throw
some light on this point, and may also deal with the question
whether the oft-recurring motive on the Roman sarcophagi
of two genii holding a cloth (parapetasma) between them, as
a background either for a scene or for the portrait of the
deceased (fig. 44), can be traced to Etruscan prototypes or
not. Hitherto, we have probably been too one-sided in
attributing the types and symbols of the plastic art of Roman
sarcophagi to Greek pictures, and the investigation of the
share of Etruria therein would be a fine subject for a mono-
graph.

XVIII

But the benevolent genii and Lasas are absolutely in the
minority in the paintings and plastic art of Etruria, and
become rarer as time goes on. The mood rises from sinister
gloom to wild terror. Two pictures will illustrate this
climax. In the Tomba del Tifone at Corneto, which was
discovered in 1832 and which is one of the grandest of the
family vaults of Etruria, there is preserved, besides the
serpent-legged demons from which the tomb has derived its
name, a large wall-painting representing the journey of a

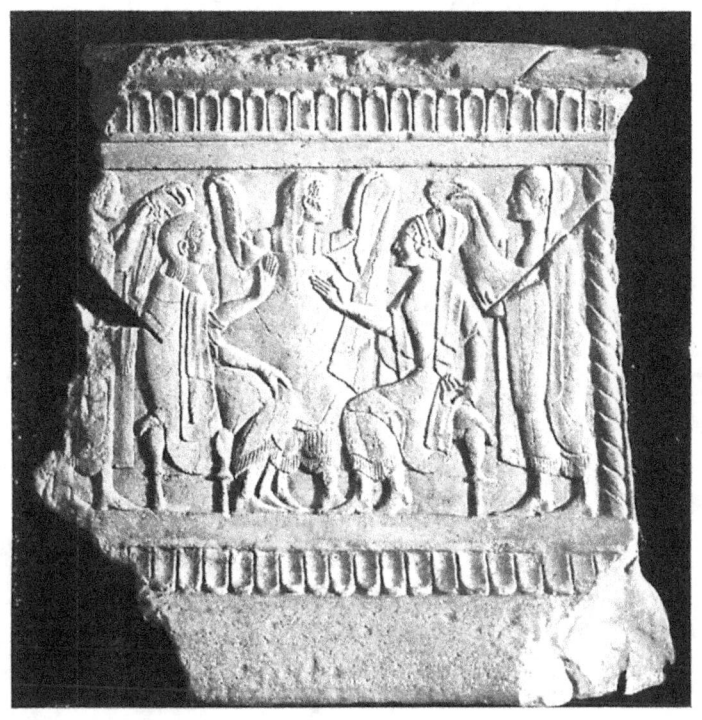

FIG. 42
RELIEF ON A TOMB ALTAR FROM CHIUSI
In the Barracco Collection in Rome

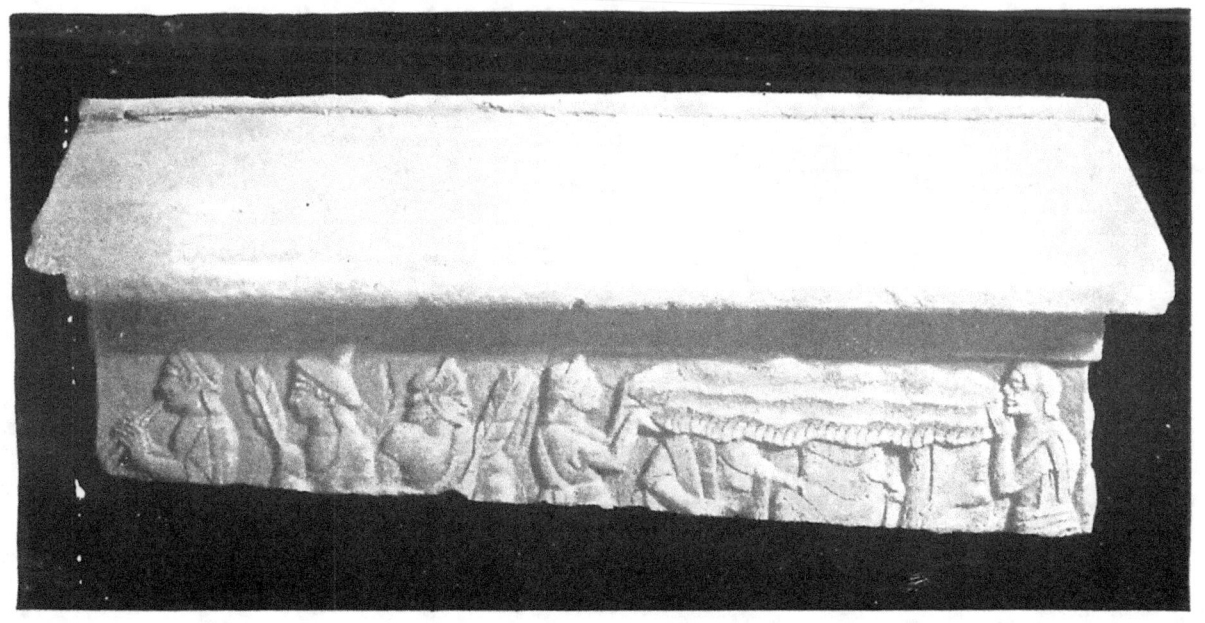

FIG. 43. CINERARY URN FROM CHIUSI

young man to the realm of the dead (fig. 45). To the left is seen an altar towards which the procession of mantle-clad youths moves ; they are led by a young demon with snakes in his hair, and a torch and a snake in his hands. The procession advances to the sound of a lituus-trumpet, and the young men carry staves and seem to be the clients of the central figure. The central figure is made conspicuous by walking without any attributes in the centre of the procession right in the front, but over his right shoulder we see Charun's clawlike hand, and Charun advances behind him like a black shadow, characterized by pointed asses' ears, snakes in his hair, and his terrible hammer. The high rank of the young man is made apparent by the inscription over his head : 'Laris Pumpus Arnthal clan cechase,' i. e. Laris Pumpus, son of Arnth, priest (*sacerdos*). Here, then, we have another of the priestly aristocrats of Etruria. After him come two more companions with staffs, and a trumpeter,[1] as well as two young men without any attributes, and the scene is terminated by some dim figures, one of which seems to be a woman with a snake in her hair and another to be of negroid type ; possibly these are the rulers of the underworld according to a later local Etruscan conception. One thing, at any rate, is plain, that the dead youth, in spite of his splendid following, goès to meet a sorrowful fate. What can the sound of the instruments avail when Charun's claw is laid on his shoulder !

This tomb dates, as far as can be judged by the style of the painting, from the first half of the fourth century B.C.[2]

[1] Trumpets at Roman funeral processions are known from reliefs on sarcophagi. *Röm. Mitt.* xxxiii. 1908, pl. iv (pp. 18–25), and Cagnat and Chabot, *Manuel d'Archéol. Romaine*, p. 586, fig. 315. Notice in the second relief from Amiternum, *Röm. Mitt.* 1908, pl. iv, at the bottom, how the banquet with the members of the family reclining on festive couches is also preserved in early Rome (second to first century B.C.).

[2] Contemporary and akin in subject is the Tomba Bruschi at Corneto. *Monumenti*, viii, pl. 36. Stryk, *Kammergräber*, p. 101. The processions here have quite a festive look ; a woman finds time to look at herself in a glass, but the devils, who appear in the crowds or lurk in the corners, show that the occasion is a serious one.

From the beginning of the next century dates the Tomba del Cardinale at Corneto, which was discovered shortly after 1760,[1] then forgotten and filled in again, and finally reopened in 1786[2] by Cardinal Garambi, bishop of Corneto. It has suffered much by exposure to wind and weather and to tourists for more than a hundred and fifty years. It has a narrow frieze with battle scenes, doubtless mythological, but the interest is centred in the long narrow frieze of pictures under the ceiling. The subject of this is the march of the shades towards the other side (fig. 46). A woman is drawn on a two-wheeled cart by two winged demons, one light and the other blue-black, both wearing the traditional garb of the genii of death, familiar from the contemporary sarcophagi and cinerary urns : a shirt with braces, and high top boots. This is perhaps the young woman who is mentioned in the inscription of the tomb : 'Ramtha, daughter of Vel and Vestreni, who was wife (*puia*) of Larth Lartha, and who lived (*valce* instead of *svalce*) nineteen years.' A young man follows in a long cloak : he turns round to a black, winged demon carrying a hammer (fig. 47). Beyond the gateway of the underworld behind him a devil of the same type is seated, and then comes a crowd of young people driven along by two devils, one of whom threatens them with his hammer.[3] A woman, who looks back moaning, is being brutally dragged along by two male demons, and at the end of the procession two winged devils are seen hastening forward, slender of limb and agile of movement, like poisonous insects. In a fragment of a frieze, which is now badly damaged, the Charun devil was once more seen in the act of crushing a skull with his hammer.[4]

This picture has a quality which reminds one of the

[1] Caylus, *Recueil d'antiquités* iv. (Paris, 1761), 112 f.

[2] Tiraboschi, *Storia della lett. ital.*, Venezia, 1795, i. 13 ff. footnote.

[3] Similar motives on tombstones and Etruscan gems. Cp. Grenier, *Bologna villanovienne et étrusque*, p.447.

Ducati, *Monumenti dei Lincei* xx. pp. 607-12. Beazley, *Lewes House Collection of Ancient Gems*, p. 33, no. 36 (pl. 3).

[4] Badly illustrated in Inghirami, *Monumenti etruschi* iv. pl. xxvii.

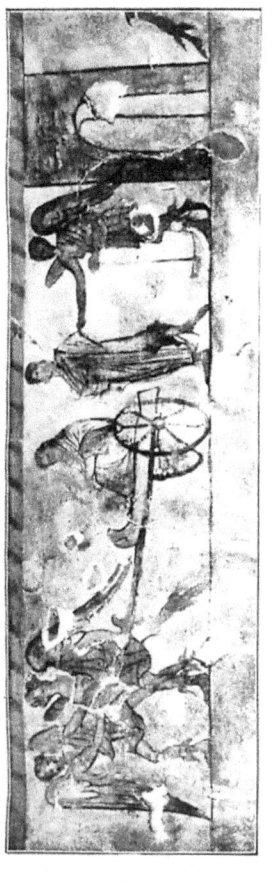

FIG. 47. PART OF THE FRIEZE IN THE TOMBA DEL CARDINALE

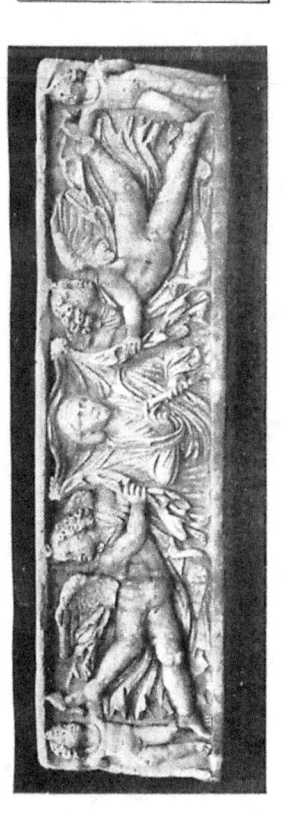

FIG. 44. ROMAN SARCOPHAGUS IN THE NY CARLSBERG GLYPTOTEK

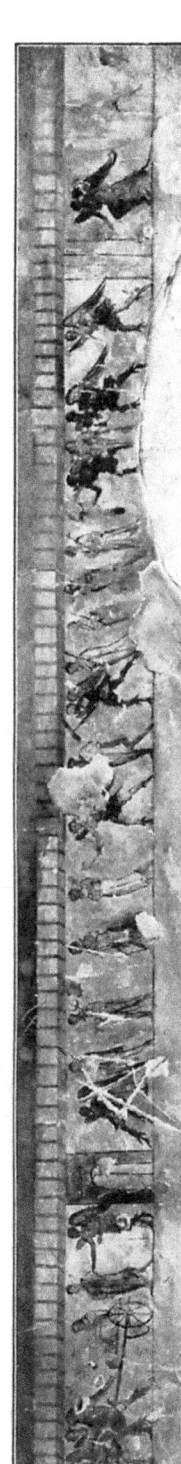

FIG. 46. PAINTED FRIEZE IN THE TOMBA DEL CARDINALE

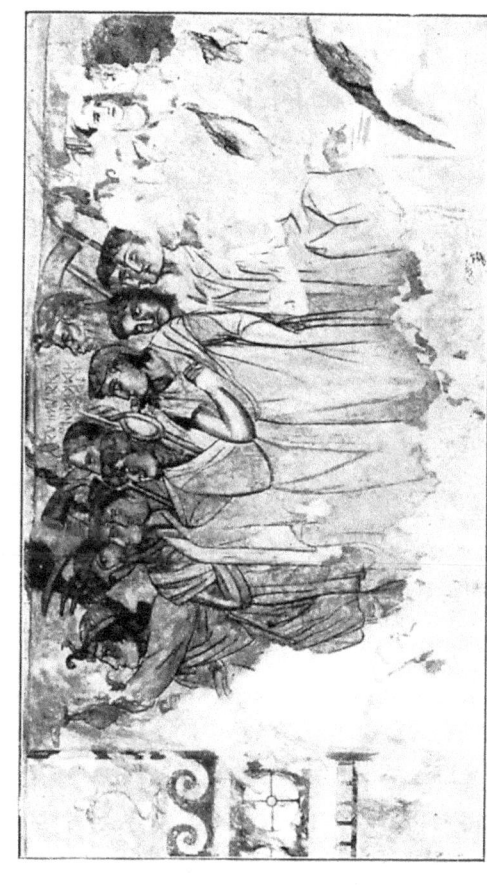

FIG. 45. PROCESSION OF THE DEAD IN THE TOMBA DEL TIFONE

frescoes in the Campo Santo at Pisa, but which is much more terrible because no hope of paradise atones for the horror. The reliefs on contemporary cinerary urns tell the same tale. To be sure, the dead reclines fat and finely bedecked on the lid of these cinerary urns, holding a drinking-bowl, or, if female, a fan. This is only tradition and has nothing to do with actual feeling. It is clear enough that the old confident conception of the hereafter as an eternal symposium has been exploded. To this the reliefs on the urns bear witness. These reliefs, if they do not directly evade the problem by choosing neutral scenes from Greek mythology, reveal a demoniac possession of appalling intensity. We need no literature in order to realize that the Etruscans under the pressure of disaster became another people, pessimistic, in terror of death, and devoid of any resiliency which would allow them to indulge in the pleasures of life. If this spiritual incubus descended upon the masses of the Roman people we can better understand how it is that the poet Lucretius can feel enthusiasm, and can arouse it in others, when he preaches the gospel of godlessness and the annihilation of the soul in death.[1] For of the Etruscan people, at any rate, the words of Lucretius [2] hold good :

Omnia perfunctus vitai praemia marces.

All that life had to give, thou hast enjoyed,
And now thou fadest.

[1] *De rerum natura* iii. 912 ff.   [2] iii. 956.

INDEX

The * indicates that the citation is in the notes.

R

Rasenas, 39.
Reclining at table, 34, 36, 57*.
Riding sideways, 27.
Rings, 32.
Rome, 45 f. *and passim.*
Rumpf, Andreas, 7 f.
Rushforth, 39*.
Ruva, 38*.

S

Salii, 18.
Samnites, 47.
Sappho, 23*, 37*.
Sarcophagi, 14, 34, 53, 55 f., 57*.
Schulze, Wilh., 39*, 45, 46*.
Scimmia, Tomba della, 25 f., 29, 45.
Scudi, Tomba degli, 34 ff., 54.
Seneca, 41*.
Shields, 8.
Skutsch, 16*.
Slaves, 41.
Soothsayers, 48.
Sophocles, 44, 54*.
Spectators, 24 f.
Stackelberg, 1, 2, 14, 20, 23, 24, 27, 28.
Stands, 24 f.
Strabo, 43*.
Struppus, 23*.

Stryk, von, 3 f.
Sunshade, 26.
Symposia, 29 ff., 37 ff., 42.

T

Tacitus, 20*.
Tapestries, 8 f.
Tarquinius, 45.
Tarquitius Priscus, 48.
Technique, 21.
Tertullian, 13*, 23.
Tevarath, 11.
Theophrastus, 19*, 34*.
Theopompus, 34*.
Theseus, 49 f.
Thomsen, Vilh., 40*.
Thucydides, 44*.
Thulin, 48*.
Thürmer, 1, 20.
Thymiaterion, 26, 39.
Tifone, Tomba del, 56 f.
Timaeus, 33*.
Tiresias, 51.
Tomba, *see the different names.*
Tonsilia tappetia, 30*.
Tori, Tomba dei, 3, 9 f., 20, 51.
Torlonia, 51.
Treasury of the Siphnians, 25.
Triclinio, Tomba del, 16 f., 20, 27, 31.
Tripudium, 18.

Triumphators, 18.
Troilus, 9.
Trumpets, 54, 57*.
Tuchulcha, 49 f.
Tusurthi, 34.
Tutulus, 22 f., 42.
Tyrrhenians, 43.

U

Urns, cinerary, 19, 30*, 34, 53, 55, 56.

V

Vanth, 52, 54.
Varro, 19, 41*, 45.
Vases, 4, 20, 22 ff.
Vasi: Tomba dei V. Dipinti, 5, 36.
Vecchio, Tomba del, 37.
Veii, 3, 7, 35, 47.
Virgil, 48*.
Vitruvius, 25.
Volnius, 45.
Vulci, 3, 51.

W

Weege, 2, 4, 6, 7, 22 ff., 27, 28, 31 f., 34.
Wigand, 26*.
Women, Etruscan, 33.
Wrestlers, 11, 15, 28.

X

Xenophanes, 19.
Xenophon, 19.

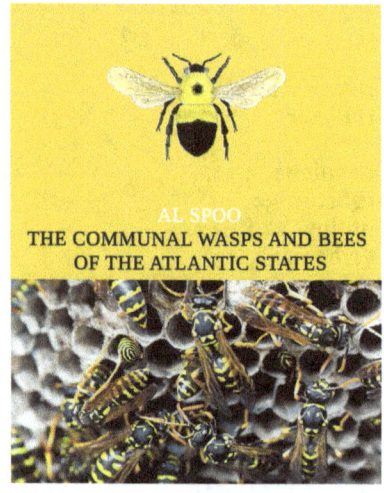

AL SPOO
THE COMMUNAL WASPS AND BEES
OF THE ATLANTIC STATES

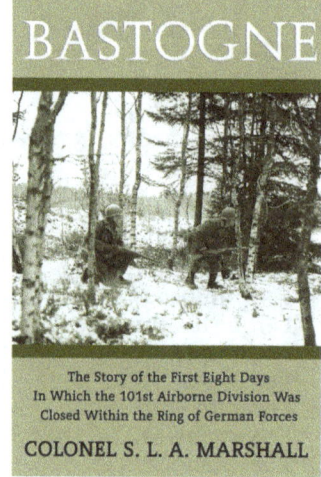

BASTOGNE

The Story of the First Eight Days
In Which the 101st Airborne Division Was
Closed Within the Ring of German Forces

COLONEL S. L. A. MARSHALL

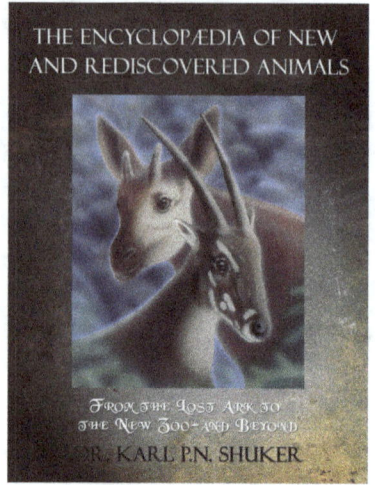

THE ENCYCLOPÆDIA OF NEW
AND REDISCOVERED ANIMALS

FROM THE LOST ARK TO
THE NEW ZOO—AND BEYOND

DR. KARL P.N. SHUKER

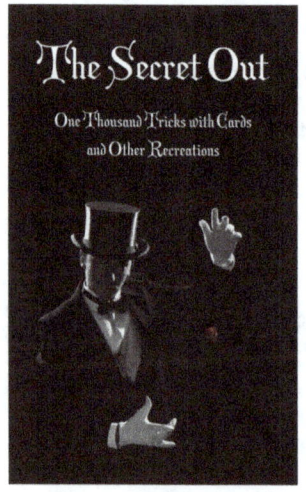

The Secret Out

One Thousand Tricks with Cards
and Other Recreations

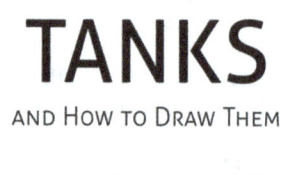

TANKS

AND HOW TO DRAW THEM

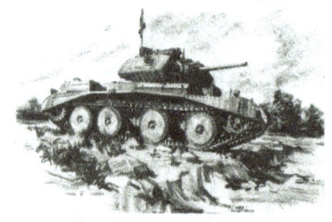

TERENCE T. CUNEO

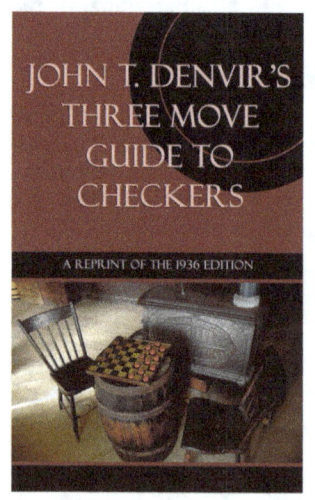

JOHN T. DENVIR'S
THREE MOVE
GUIDE TO
CHECKERS

A REPRINT OF THE 1936 EDITION

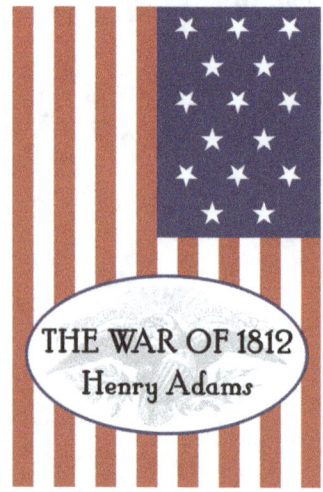

THE WAR OF 1812
Henry Adams

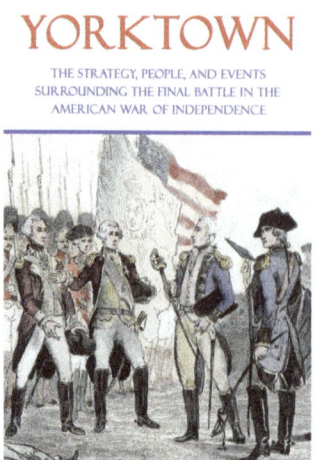

YORKTOWN

THE STRATEGY, PEOPLE, AND EVENTS
SURROUNDING THE FINAL BATTLE IN THE
AMERICAN WAR OF INDEPENDENCE

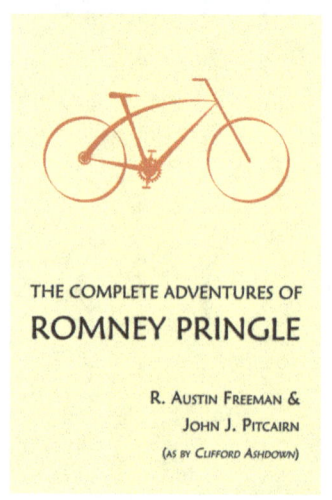

THE COMPLETE ADVENTURES OF
ROMNEY PRINGLE

R. AUSTIN FREEMAN &
JOHN J. PITCAIRN
(AS BY CLIFFORD ASHDOWN)

Coachwhip Publications
CoachwhipBooks.com

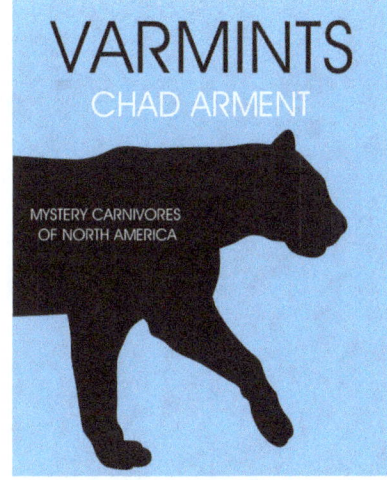

VARMINTS
CHAD ARMENT
MYSTERY CARNIVORES OF NORTH AMERICA

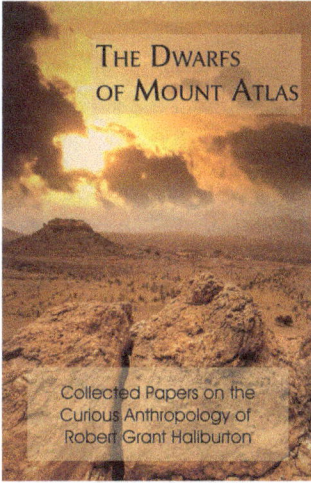

THE DWARFS OF MOUNT ATLAS
Collected Papers on the Curious Anthropology of Robert Grant Haliburton

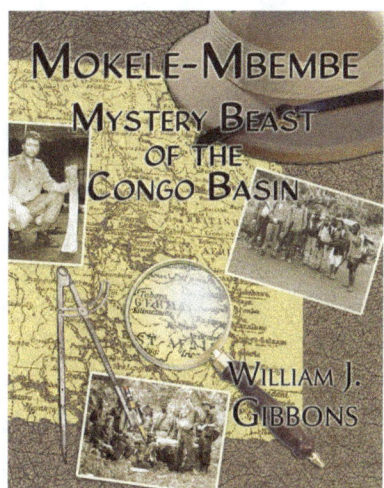

MOKELE-MBEMBE
MYSTERY BEAST OF THE CONGO BASIN
WILLIAM J. GIBBONS

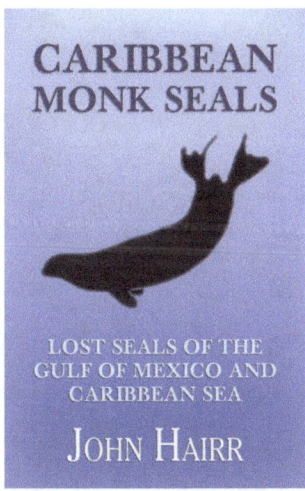

CARIBBEAN MONK SEALS
LOST SEALS OF THE GULF OF MEXICO AND CARIBBEAN SEA
JOHN HAIRR

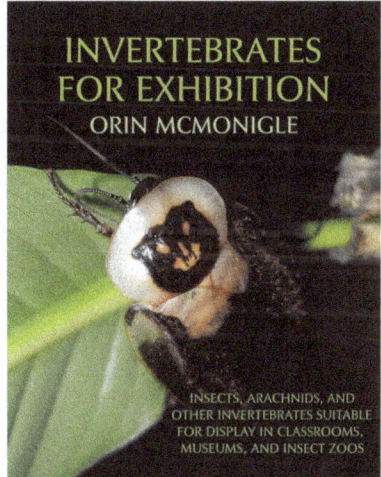

INVERTEBRATES FOR EXHIBITION
ORIN MCMONIGLE
INSECTS, ARACHNIDS, AND OTHER INVERTEBRATES SUITABLE FOR DISPLAY IN CLASSROOMS, MUSEUMS, AND INSECT ZOOS

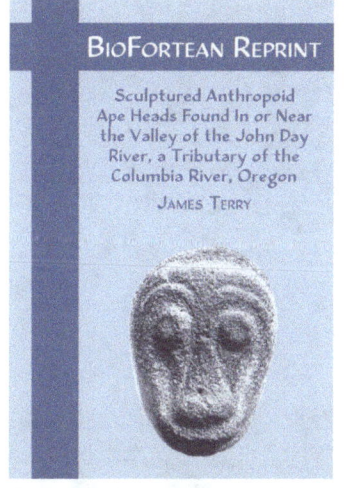

BioFortean Reprint
Sculptured Anthropoid Ape Heads Found In or Near the Valley of the John Day River, a Tributary of the Columbia River, Oregon
JAMES TERRY

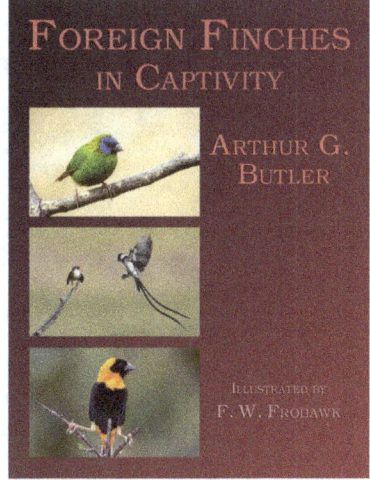

FOREIGN FINCHES IN CAPTIVITY
ARTHUR G. BUTLER
ILLUSTRATED BY F. W. FROHAWK

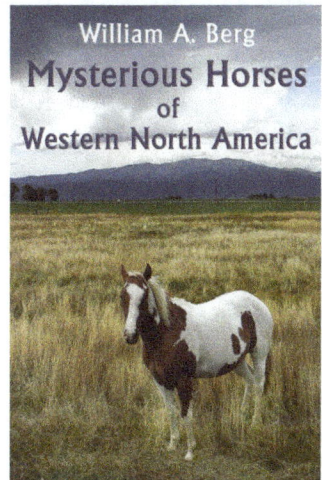

William A. Berg
Mysterious Horses of Western North America

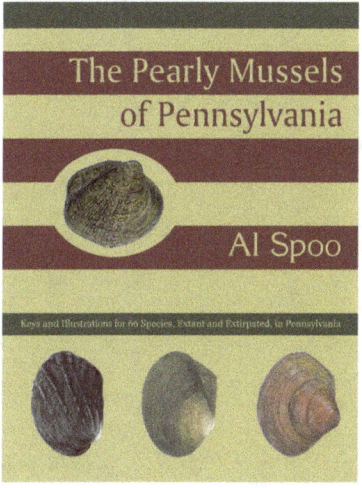

The Pearly Mussels of Pennsylvania
Al Spoo
Keys and Illustrations for 66 Species, Extant and Extirpated, in Pennsylvania